The Best is Yet to Come

John Glass

Acknowledgements

Many thanks to those who have read and advised on the manuscript and especially to David and Jan Holdaway for their part in the production of this book.

Contact John Glass at: jjglass@me.com

ISBN 978-1-907929-77-9

www.lifepublications.org.uk

Dedication

To June Freudenberg, Diane Druce and the team of intercessors at Barnet Christian Fellowship who prayed daily for Marilyn and I during the sixteen years I was General Superintendent.

Commendations

John Glass has been at the forefront of Christian leadership for over two decades. His influence and ministry has been felt and appreciated way beyond the Elim Pentecostal Churches which he served as General Superintendent for 16 years.

This book brings John's unique perspective and insight on the factors and events that have shaped his life and ministry in the journey from seasons as pastor of local and city churches, church planter, author and broadcaster to the challenges of leading a denominational and cross denominational organisations.

As well as sharing stirring and inspirational stories of God's grace John continues his lifelong passion for calling forth the gifts and ministries of others.

Chris Cartwright
General Superintendent Elim Church

Packed with invaluable leadership lessons and inspiring faith stories, I am left with a greater hunger for God and deeply challenged by the reality of the Holy Spirit's leading in John's life. I found myself crying, laughing and praying as I read. An absolute must read for every leader!

Steve Uphall
Senior Pastor, All Nations Church, Wolverhampton

The Best is Yet to Come

Having known John for very many years now I am delighted to be able to recommend his autobiography and am certain it will both challenge and inspire every reader. This is a 'must read' particularly for every Pentecostal Christian, although its insightful stories and anecdotes mean that everyone will benefit from the truths it contains.

Thank you John for putting pen to paper and providing us with this exceptional account of a life dedicated to Christ, together with the clear proof from your personal testimony that *"the steps of a good man are ordered and directed by the Lord."*

John Partington
National Leader Assemblies of God GB

This wonderful autobiography exposes the true passions and personality of the life of a man devoted to serving Jesus and his generation.

Several years ago, in the first mentoring session I had with John I knew, instinctively, I must not be late. I arrived at the restaurant ten minutes early but he was already there. I was engulfed in his generosity and wisdom from the outset. He poured himself into the then rookie pastor. Ironically, I didn't feel rushed but this great man gave me all the time I needed.

This book captures that essence and will mentor you, too. John's desire to grow bigger people will rub off on you. Your 'inscape' will expand as you turn each page. Enjoy.

Simon Jarvis
Senior Leader, One Church Network

Spanning six decades from some of the earliest days of the Elim Movement to the present time, John Glass offers a warm and engaging account of his life and ministry. His personal reflections are replete with intriguing anecdotes, soaked in spiritual truth and rich in leadership insights.

The Best is Yet to Come

John Glass held Elim's highest office for the longest time in recent history and the integrity, passion and wisdom he brought to that role shines through these pages. I recommend this book not just as a slice of Elim history but as a primer for all those who aspire to Christian service of the highest order.

Colin Dye
Leader of Kensington Temple / London City Church

I've known John Glass for more than forty years. We are close friends, and I love and respect him more than I can express. Having reached the top position in Elim, he has now shared his heart with all of us. Every person attending an Elim church will want to read this book. You will come away thanking God for giving Elim such a statesman as this *"for such a time as this"*.

Lyndon Bowring
Executive Chairman CARE

Contents

The Best is Yet to Come

Foreword

I am so honoured to be invited to write this foreword. One of the most thrilling providences of my entire pilgrimage has been the Elim Pentecostal Church coming into my life and the way I have felt loved and accepted by the Elim people ever since.

I have known every General Superintendent of Elim for the past forty years. Eldin Corsie, Wynne Lewis and John Glass became good friends. And now to be asked to write the Foreword to John Glass's autobiography is like a seal on my relationship with Elim.

I will never forget the feeling that came over me the moment I stepped onto the premises at Bognor Regis many years ago where Elim was holding its annual conference. I was not prepared for this. As I walked around the area, noticing the people I had not yet personally met, I felt myself saying, "I am home". I didn't know why, but that was the exact feeling that came over me then. But I know why now.

As a speaker at that meeting I felt totally at one with the people. It was there that Lyndon Bowring became a close friend. It was through Lyndon that I got to know Eldin, Wynne, John and eventually Colin Dye, senior pastor of Kensington Temple. Colin, Lyndon and I began praying for each other – plus all our families – every day. But that was only the beginning. Since our retirement from Westminster Chapel in 2002, my friendship with Colin and Kensington Temple grew stronger and stronger. For the past four years Louise and I have been a part of the staff at KT, spending some six months a year with them. This also allowed for us to have further fellowship and ministry with the wider Elim family and especially John Glass who has kindly invited me to speak at different functions many times.

I was gripped with John Glass's book from the first page. I could not help feeling as I read this book how God has prepared John – right from the very beginning – and throughout his life for such a time as this. He was brought up in a strong Pentecostal home. There is no doubt that God had His hand on John from the start. He was being groomed for leadership from his earliest days. You will be enthralled with John's depictions of his pilgrimage and encouraged to see how God refines one's gift through trials and tribulations.

Influenced by certain Puritan books that reflect the providence of God, as well as some of the writings of Dr Martyn Lloyd-Jones, John demonstrates wisdom as he takes us through his personal life chronologically. He never promoted himself to positions he held. God put him where he was to be. His life is an example to those who enter the ministry hoping for prestigious positions. John's example is an implicit rebuke to ambitious people who angle for places. This book is a reminder that God is the one who promotes. *"No one from the east or the west or from the desert can exalt a man. But it is God who judges: He brings one down, he exalts another,"* (Psalm 75:6-7).

You may well enjoy reading about the petty quarrels that come up when in pastoral leadership – whether about music style, how much to watch television, dealing with different cultures, prophetic words or difficult personalities! Being prepared to become a future General Superintendent of Elim involves all sorts of challenges for the day; one must be a gentle diplomat twenty-four hours a day – which is what John turned out to be.

You will delight in reading about his relationship with his wife, Marilyn. He reveals how he trusts her instincts. His love and admiration for her comes through every time he mentions her. There is nothing that challenges a marriage like the ministry. A good way to test the quality of a man is by what he says about his wife. God's esteem of a leader is not their preaching ability or diplomatic skills but the kind of spouse or parent one is.

Every young person thinking about going into the ministry must read this book. Every pastor of any denomination will profit from this book. Every Elim member should read this book and will gain a fresh appreciation of the Elim Pentecostal Church. You will gain a perspective of what it means to be a leader. You will come away feeling God's hand has not only been on John Glass through these years but the Elim Movement as well.

RT Kendall

The Best is Yet to Come

1

Early Life

Number 309 Dickinson Road, Manchester is dilapidated now but in the early 1950s was a grand house. It had thirteen large rooms and one of my earliest memories is of my mother arranging for a Union Jack to be hoisted from a pole that was accessible from one of the windows of the billiard room on the top floor in order to celebrate the coronation of the young Queen Elizabeth II. A wide red-carpeted staircase with brass rods at every step accessed the various levels. The most memorable area being the dining room with its large table around which thirty guests could be accommodated. Fifteen years later I would sit around that same table as a student which, a couple of sections having been removed, my parents gave to the Elim Bible College in Capel. It remained in the library and second year lecture hall for as long at the college remained in Surrey.

My father, who his friends called Jack, was born Jacob Troughton Glass. He was one of seven brothers born to James and Elizabeth Glass who farmed in Loughall, Armagh in Northern Ireland. Pre-dating the birth of the modern Pentecostal Movement they belonged to a group referred to as the 'Holy Rollers' due to their demonstrative style of worship. Their view of faith would seem as extreme today as it was then. Elizabeth, for example, would not take medication when ill believing that Jesus alone was her divine healer. It is said that when suffering from appendicitis she would take nothing at all for the relief of the pain. She lived well into her nineties and as a young woman attended the church in Monaghan, the first to be established by George Jeffreys, the founder of the

Elim Pentecostal churches. There is nothing particularly remarkable about this other than the fact that the person who was to be the principle female soloists in Jeffreys' crusades would be my maternal grandmother, Alice Woodhead (nee Fisher) and one of my most treasured possessions to this day is a 78rpm disc which has George Jeffreys preaching on one side and my grandmother singing on the other. That was cutting edge media in those days and a hundred years after the recording was made I took a photo of the newly formed *'Elim Sound'* musicians as they handled these recordings for the first time.

My great-grandfather Isaac Fisher, his wife and four girls of which Alice was one, were members of the Salvation Army in Dinnington near Sheffield. He was a coal miner in the days when it was a difficult and dangerous occupation. When he came into the experience of the 'Baptism in the Holy Spirit' and came to believe that the Gifts of the Spirit, including speaking in tongues, did not cease at the birth of the Early Church he was asked to leave the 'Army'. He later became a trustee of Silverdale Hall, one of the first Assemblies of God fellowships. He was in his nineties when as a small boy I visited his small terraced miner's cottage situated in the same village where he had worked all his life. He was an almost patriarchal figure in my mind. I never saw him without a three piece suit on with a watch chain in his waist coat and I never heard him speak for very long without mentioning the Lord Jesus during the conversation.

John Woodhead, who later married one of his daughters, Alice, and was to be my maternal grandfather and become one of the greatest influences on my life, was born in the mining village of Mosborough almost opposite where the current Elim church is situated. At the outbreak of the First World War, having lied about his age in order to enlist, he was injured twice in the Battle of the Somme before he was officially old enough to be present on the battlefield. He was one of the few survivors of the battle of Devil's Wood.

After his conversion he sought the Baptism of the Spirit for some period without success. His father-in-law, Isaac Fisher, realised that the problem he was struggling with was not theological but intellectual. He was trying to reason everything out and this was becoming a stumbling block. Isaac laid his hands on him one evening with the prayer, "Lord, chop his 'ed off" and within moments my grandfather was filled with the Holy Spirit and began speaking in tongues.

John became an evangelist with Assemblies of God and, when George Jeffreys had more invitations around the country than he could accept, my grandfather was loaned to the newly formed Elim Movement. He never returned. Over twenty churches now in our Movement were pioneered by him during that period.

The normal procedure was for him to conduct tent crusades the converts of which were the basis of the new church plant. Remarkable miracles of divine healing took place during that time and it was in one of those tent meetings that I committed my life to Christ – but more of that later. John Woodhead, after who I am named, spent the remainder of his ministry pastoring churches within the Movement and in 1960 was elected as President of Elim – a position that was held for the period of a year and which was discontinued in 1989.

My father, Jack, married Eileen, one of John and Alice's two daughters. Jack had enlisted in the army in the Second World War and joined the Eighth Army, known as the Desert Rats, under Field Marshal Montgomery. When discharged he did not return to Ireland but moved to England and served as an apprentice in the printing industry. By the time I was born he had a small printing business of his own and also owned a couple of greengrocer shops. Although by no means wealthy he was sufficiently successful to be able to purchase the house alluded to earlier and to employ a maid/nanny to assist my mother in the upkeep of the house and care for the children. This life-style was, however, soon to change.

It was while living in this large house that two events within the first five years of my life were to shape my future more than any other event in the years that would follow.

My grandfather, John Woodhead, was conducting a crusade in Salford near Manchester. Marquees were usually erected in fields but there were occasions when this was not possible. The most well-known circus in those days was Chipperfield's and, when the advertised circus programme had concluded, he arranged that while the tent was erected and the seating and lighting was in place he would rent the arena for a *'Revival and Divine Healing Crusade'*.

To see a platform erected in the middle of a sawdust ring was surreal. George Jeffreys also adopted an entrepreneurial approach to securing large venues. When looking for the biggest venue in Liverpool he booked the boxing arena in Lime Street – the photo of which can be seen in Elim's centenary publication *Defining Moments.*

Salford, near Manchester, was a heavily industrialised area made famous by the LS Lowry paintings of that period. These were the days before the *Clean Air Act* and it is said that the birds in Salford coughed rather than sang. The tent in Salford was erected on a disused car park.

I was around the age of five when my mother took me to hear my grandfather preach. More than sixty years later I still retain a vivid memory of that meeting. My mind easily conjures up the rows of wooden chairs and the towering tent poles. I can still hear the flapping sides of the tent that, however well rigged, responded noisily to every gust of wind or shower of rain.

The gospel could not have been presented more simply that night. In essence I heard that everyone had done wrong and the bible called that sin. There was nothing that we could do to avert the punishment for sin that everyone deserved. However, God sent his son in the person of Jesus to live in our world and to die on the cross. If we confessed our sin, and put our trust in Christ who stands in our place, then God the Father grants us forgiveness on the basis of what his son Jesus had done.

When the service concluded my grandfather, on leaving the platform and passing by the row in which I and my mother sat, noticed that I was crying. He immediately came to a wrong conclusion. He had been aware that I, among many others, mostly adults, had raised my hand as the hymn *Just As I Am* was being sung.

In his services everyone who made a decision was given a New Testament and he had assumed that his grandson was in tears because he had not been given his copy. But that was not why I was crying. Though just a child I had understood, and was overwhelmed by, what Jesus had done for me on the cross. Even at the age of five I remember feeling somewhat 'put out' that my grandfather had thought otherwise.

My grandfather's crusade years saw the emergence of many young people several of which would later become significant leaders in the Elim Movement.

On one occasion as he concluded preaching at a church service and was exiting via the minor hall he heard what was known then as *Elim Choruses* being played on a piano. He told me many years later that it was not just the brilliant musicianship that drew his attention, but the large crowd of young people that had gathered around the piano and were enthusiastically singing.

Making his way to the front he saw a handsome young man in a soldier's uniform at the keyboard and subsequently invited him to be his crusade pianist. Eldin Corsie, who later married Vivienne Kennedy, the daughter of Elim pastor James Craig Kennedy, would become one of the earliest pastors of Elim's largest church Kensington Temple, be the principal of the Bible College and eventually the General Superintendent of the Movement.

Another young man who joined the crusade party as song leader and pianist was John Lancaster who later became one of the most respected leaders in our Movement. Like Eldin he served on Elim's Executive Council (now called National Leadership Team). For many years John pastored the large church in Bridge Street, Leeds and served as Elim's Director of Publications.

John Lancaster tells the story that, on the evening my parents had invited him and his young lady to have a meal with them at 309 Dickinson Road, he chose that occasion to propose to Dorothy. They were married for 63 years and she went home to be with the Lord in 2014. Both of these men would become a huge influence, not just on myself, but on generations of Elim leaders.

The second life changing moment in the first five years of my life also happened at the large house in Manchester.

The day could not have commenced in a more ordinary way. I was getting dressed to go down for breakfast and was standing facing the bedroom door. The ceilings of the house were high and that meant that there was a large area between the top of the door lintel and the ceiling. It was into that space that a vision, of what I instinctively knew was the form of the Lord Jesus, appeared. I had no sense of alarm or fear but what affected me most were what I considered to be the 'strange clothes' that he was wearing. The image began to fade from the head to the feet and left me with no recollection of the face at all.

Approaching the breakfast table I told my mother that I had 'seen Jesus' in the bedroom. Her response was simply to ask me what he was wearing. I said that I thought the clothes were strange and, having described them, she informed me that these were the high-priestly clothes as described in the Old Testament. She told me that Jesus was our High Priest. When I asked how she knew about the clothes she said that her father, my grandfather, had had exactly the same vision when the Lord had called him into the ministry.

It was from that moment that I concluded one day I would be a pastor. I do not recollect my parents telling that story to anyone else subsequently nor did we discuss it ever again. I assumed that they must have told my grandparents but, as they never raised the matter with me either, I cannot be sure.

2

Chorlton

My early childhood was a happy one growing up in Manchester with my parents and my two younger sisters Alison and Susan. However, not long after the events outlined in the last chapter our lives and lifestyle changed.

Elim contacted my father, who was a businessman not a pastor, and asked if he would look after a small group of five people who wanted to see an Elim church commenced in their area. The idea, I assume, was that he would look after them for a few months while a pioneer crusade was arranged. However, the crusade never materialised and my father ended up pioneering the church himself and led the congregation in Chorlton-cum-Hardy, South Manchester for over twenty years.

The small group initially met in the upstairs storeroom of a corner shop which, being less than ideal, motivated them to begin praying for a building of their own.

One day, my father was driving through Chorlton when his car appeared to have broken down. This had never happened previously so he got out to lift the bonnet and investigate the problem. Finding no apparent reason for the breakdown he put the bonnet back down and, when preparing to try the ignition again, noticed two properties across the road. One was a house and the other a hall. The frontage was so overgrown with trees that, had he not stopped, he would not have seen the sign that revealed that the properties were for sale. He took down the phone number of the agent, got into the car, turned on the ignition and immediately the engine burst into life.

The small group were not able to raise the money and Elim Headquarters were unable to help. This, therefore, meant that the big house would have to be sold. The country was in recession, however, and thirteen-roomed houses were not easy to dispose of.

A long period went by without any interest being shown in the property. Eventually an offer was made at way below the market value and my father shook hands on the deal. Within days of that happening Granada TV, based in Manchester, approached him and told him that they wanted to purchase. They offered him a great deal of money but he responded by saying the property was no longer on the market.

The reason they wanted it, they told him, was that their top entertainers were being put in expensive city centre hotels and they wanted a facility they could manage themselves that, even after conversion, would be saving them a huge amount every year.

They were staggered to learn that my father defined 'off the market' as a handshake and the giving of his word. No legal transaction had been entered into and no paperwork signed. He refused to budge and consequently the house went for the far lower price.

We, as a family, moved into the small house and work began on turning the adjacent property into a church. The greengrocer businesses had been sold and my father's only income now was from the small printing business.

Although finances were not discussed in front of the children we knew enough to realise that things were not easy during those days. Combined with this my mother was in less than good health. The year was 1954. Even though Elim Headquarters had not supported him in those early years my father handed over the deeds of the house and the church to them once everything had been paid for.

Chorlton

My father and grandfather could not have been more different. My grandfather was well known as an evangelist and church planter and pastored many of Elim's largest churches while my father was essentially a businessman who was in ministry for eleven years before even applying for ordination. He pastored one of the Movement's smallest churches and rarely took ministry engagements outside his own congregation. My mother, on the other hand, was often in demand as a soloist and speaker at women's events.

Having said this, both my father and grandfather had a profound influence upon me. From my father I learned the importance of integrity in ministry. Growing up in a small church forever gave me an appreciation of the particular struggles in building from a narrow base and very much influenced my attitude to smaller churches in later years when I was elected as a Regional Leader, and later General Superintendent. All the secretaries and PAs who worked for me when I occupied those roles knew that I would never decline an invitation to a small church in favour of a larger one. I had very little concern for the concept of 'preaching opportunities' but simply wanted to be engaged in a ministry where my involvement would hopefully make the greatest difference.

Up to the age of ten I attended a primary school a few hundred yards away from where our house and church was situated in Oswald Road. Between the house and the school was a butcher's shop and, when I was a little older, rather than augmenting my pocket money with a paper round I delivered meat to customers on a Saturday riding a heavy, black metal bike with a wicker basket in the front. One of the regular customers was Doris Speed who played the landlady Annie Walker in *Coronation Street*. I remember her mostly for the size of her tip which was the lowest on the round – a threepenny bit (1p). I received ten shillings a week (50p) for my Saturday job and this was the point at which I commenced tithing.

Our house did not have central heating though the church next door was heated with a coke fire. My father would rise early on a Sunday morning to light the boiler situated in an outhouse at the end of our garden and adjacent to the church. One of my jobs on a Sunday was to keep the fire stoked, and this exercise was repeated for the Tuesday prayer meeting and Wednesday Bible Study.

I was baptised in water at the age of ten at which point my parents gave me my first Bible. I still have it – together with all the other Bibles I have used over the years and, during my time as General Superintendent, they were stacked on a shelf in my office in Malvern eliciting memories of the various stages of my ministry and the faithfulness of God throughout those periods.

A year later, on a visit to my grandparents – by this time my grandfather, John Woodhead, was approaching the end of his ministry and pastoring the Elim Church in York – I learned via the Sunday morning announcements that a 'waiting meeting' would be held for those who were seeking the Baptism in the Holy Spirit and that this would take place at the close of the evening service.

I asked my grandfather if I could attend and he agreed. That night I was filled with the Spirit and spoke in tongues for the first time.

This event coincided with my moving on to my new school as, having passed the entrance exam, I donned the green blazer of the local Grammar School.

The effect of the Baptism in the Spirit was that I now wanted to share my faith at every possible opportunity. The first person I led to Christ was a friend called Alan Jones who had moved with me to the new school. We immediately donned a small gold cross in our blazers in order to create initial conversation opportunities.

At the age of fourteen I asked the boy in the next desk what he was going to do over the school holidays. When he told me he had no plans I suggested that he come with me to what was to be the first Fraisthorpe Youth Camp – now called Elim Festival.

It was there that he committed his life to Christ and remained a friend throughout my school years later becoming a teacher and an Elder at the Elim Church in Glossop.

Fifty years later, when attending an Elim church while on holiday, and the pastor having acknowledged that the General Superintendent was in the meeting, a man in his twenties who had been sitting next to me said, "My father knows you. He once told me that he went to school with you." Here was the now married son of the 14-year-old boy I had witnessed to those years earlier. Someone once said, "Anyone can count the number of seeds in an apple but no one can predict the number of apples in a seed." It is not just the person you bring to Christ that matters, but the influence that person has on the countless number of people that he or she influences in their lifetime.

I often think of the American Evangelist Mordecai Ham in this regard. At the conclusion of a crusade that had brought little results, a newspaper reporter wrote that Ham must be feeling somewhat disappointed, if not depressed, with the lack of responses to his preaching. Undoubtedly the reporter was right. What no one realised was that among the tiny handful of young men that came to the front during that crusade was Billy Graham – someone who would lead countless thousands to Christ through his preaching.

Sadly, rarely do our spiritual lives continue on an ever upward ascent. The graph that charts our progress has its troughs as well as its peaks. Mine was to be no exception.

I had been top of my class in my last year in junior school and had secured a place at Grammar School. However, as my O Levels approached I was going through an all too typical teenage phase. I was still attending church but in a poor state spiritually. I told my parents that I could not possibly attend the two mid-week meetings as I had so much homework to do. However, as soon as they left for the church next door, and I heard the first hymn being sung, I closed my books and put on the then black and white TV and would watch programmes such as *That Was The Week That Was* hosted by a young David Frost. My father would put his hand on the TV on returning from church to see if it was still warm (they had valves in those days) but I had timed and planned my deception to perfection.

Unsurprisingly my chickens came home to roost. I failed all of the nine O Levels that I took – even including Religious Knowledge.

On one occasion while reluctantly sitting in church waiting for the service to start my father was about to pass by me on his way to the pulpit. I was sitting at the end of the row near the aisle and he bent down to whisper in my ear, "I have no idea whether or not one day you will become a pastor, but if you do I hope that no one sits in your church looking as miserable as you are doing in mine."

I would like to say that my spiritual wake-up call came through a powerful spiritual experience. It did not. It came about by my headmaster deciding to hand me my exam results in person and the subsequent awareness that I had let my parents down. This was the primary factor that kick-started me into re-evaluating my life and the direction I was heading.

During the interim period between school ending and my results coming out I had applied for a job in the city of Manchester. I honestly harboured the illusion that I would get at least seven of the nine O Levels I had taken and expressed as much at my interview. I secured the position on that basis and when the results came out had to tell my employer that my expectations had not materialised. Remarkably, the company said that as they were pleased with my performance in the short time that I had been with them, they were going to take the unusual step of retaining me without the required entrance qualifications.

Prior to entering Bible College I worked for the American finance company General Motors Acceptance Corporation. When I handed in my notice the General Manager expressed disappointment that I was leaving – largely because of the amount of training that they had afforded me. In an attempt to ameliorate the situation I suggested someone who they may be willing to consider as my possible successor – someone who I had recently led to the Lord and with far more academic qualifications than I had.

He applied, secured the role and worked alongside me in it for a month before I left. However, just one year later he too handed in his notice in order to enter Elim Bible College and later became an Elim minister. Keith was later to be best man at my wedding and I at his. Though there were no entrance qualifications needed for the Bible College I took three O Levels – Maths, English and Religious Knowledge externally – and secured them just to prove to myself, and possibly others, that I was able to do so.

One week before setting off for Bible College I came home late from work and went straight to the prayer meeting which was already in progress. Looking for a place to sit, I saw that a young man around my age was present who I had never seen in church before though his face was vaguely familiar.

At the conclusion of the service it transpired that we had not only been to the same Grammar School but also played in the same school orchestra – I on the cello and he on the trombone. We had never been in the same circle of friends as I was in the fifth form and he in the sixth. He went on to relate that he had gone on to university and, through the witness of the local Christian Union, had committed his life to Christ. I, of course, congratulated him but said that we would not be able to get to know one another any better as the following week I was off to Bible College. "That's remarkable," he responded, "I have applied for a Bible college too and leave next week". Both of us not only attended the same college but had been allocated to share the same room during our first year. Within just two years the small church in Chorlton had five students attending Elim Bible College.

After my father retired from the church in south Manchester a succession of ministers were appointed each of whom reduced the church numerically before they left not only the church but also the ministry.

My parents watched the continual demise of the church they had founded from their retirement in Southport and it seemed at one point as if the church may even close. This was until Paul and Mags Hallam were appointed. Though they inherited the house and the church, they had only a very small nucleus of people to work with. Through their tenacity, hard work and sacrificial lifestyle they have built a phenomenal church. It was a joy to speak at the opening of their new church facility that is now located next to Media City in Salford, has a congregation of over four hundred and international expressions of the church in India and Romania.

3

Elim Bible College

I was still only nineteen years of age when I entered Elim Bible College – situated in those days in Capel, Surrey, in fourteen acres of manicured lawns in a village between Dorking and Horsham. In retrospect they were two of the happiest years of my life. Many of the students I met in those days became lifelong friends and around seventeen of those who entered the Elim ministry in that two year period served the Movement throughout the remainder of their entire working life.

Two people with whom I shared a room towards the end of my first year were Geoff Feasey and Gordon Neale – both of them would go on to be outstanding Regional Leaders and serve alongside me on the National Leadership Team.

The academic standards of those years were not as high as they are today and the majority of input was directed to preparing students for a pastoral role within the Elim Movement. Most people, unless of course they were language students, were solely in college for that purpose.

The effect of living in and adjusting to a closed community, usually with three or four students to a room, was an education in itself.

The fees for the two years were partially covered by a grant from the education authority and for the first couple of terms I was able to cover the shortfall from the modest savings that I had accumulated while working at GMAC. I knew that I would have to find work in the holidays and what could not be gleaned from that source would have to be 'prayed in'.

There was a point at which it was announced that all students would need to purchase a specific set of books in time for a new course that would commence on the following Monday. It was Friday and I had no money at all left in my account. As I had made it a matter of principle not to share with my parents, or anyone else, what my financial position was my only hope was that in the following day's post something would arrive to meet the necessary cost.

In those days post was allocated to alphabetically labelled pigeon holes. There was only one post on a Saturday so I was present as soon as the letters arrived. It quickly became clear that there was no post for me. I waited for a while until everyone had retrieved their post in order to see if a letter had been wrongly allocated to someone else's section. It had not.

That afternoon I spent some time in prayer and subsequently felt I should go downstairs to the letter rack. This seemed implausible as, given there was no second post, there was little point. However the impression continued and, obeying this prompting, I went to my allocated pigeon hole to find a manila envelope with my name on it, clearly posted internally as there was neither address nor stamp. Inside was precisely the amount of money I needed.

In my first holiday break a short term job was not easy to find. In fact the only one that could be secured was working for the retail outlet in which my sister, Alison, was the manager.

On the first day back at college it was customary that at the first student meeting testimonies were called for as to how we had spent our time. I did not contribute. However, the Principal for some reason singled me out in front of everyone and asked if I had secured a job as I had hoped. I answered in the affirmative hoping he would not proceed further. Unfortunately he did by asking, "So where did you find work?"

To the rapturous delight of all present I had to respond, "The outlet for babies and young children – *Mothercare*."

In the summer recess it was clear that I would need to secure a substantial amount of money and asked a friend in Manchester to look out for something on my behalf. There were just two stipulations. The first was that it should pay as much as possible and the second, naturally, that it was legal.

On arriving home from college I was told that both stipulations had been met but that I may not be entirely comfortable with the solution. The job secured was the 'third man' on a dray for Scottish Newcastle Breweries. Every lorry had a driver and his mate and the 'third man' was casual labour who did all the heavy lifting. In some cases the full metal casks had to be carried shoulder high up several flights of stairs. I lost a stone in weight in the first three weeks but emerged from the ordeal at the end of the summer recess a good deal stronger and fitter.

I was with a different 'run' every day and resolved to witness to every team every time I was with them – something that I managed to do throughout the whole of the summer. When I collected my wages, which were substantial and covered my entire fees for the next two terms, I was approached to see if I was willing to be employed in the following Christmas break.

On one of those deliveries it seemed that for the first time the opportunity might not arise for me to share my faith but I resolved not to break my record and decided that I would do so one way or another on the way back. It was a bitterly cold and snowy day and we had driven to a pub in a small town on the outskirts of Manchester.

The normal procedure was that, the delivery being complete, the driver and his mate would have a pint with the landlord and, as I did not drink, I would sit in the cab waiting their return. On this occasion they seemed to be away for an inordinately long period of time and, when they eventually materialised and climbed into the cab alongside me, they handed me an envelope stuffed with pound notes.

My first thought was that this was their annual Christmas bonus and I was surprised on two counts. The first was that they would be sharing this with me as it was the fruit of twelve months work and I was a temporary employee. The second was the amount of money involved.

When I declined on the basis of the first point the solution to the second conundrum quickly became clear. They were involved in a scam against the brewery with the pub.

When I continued to decline the driver said, "Why would you not want the money, you're a student aren't you?" The driver's mate then asked, "What is it exactly that you are studying?" When I replied, "Theology," they both joined in with "Oh… (expletives) we have been trying to implicate a vicar in our scam." What at first seemed to be the worst opportunity to witness eventually turned out to be one of the best.

On my return to college I considered it highly unlikely that I would be singled out again to share where I had been working but I was wrong. I was tempted to respond that my fees had been met by "a movement of the spirit" but shared the plain facts which were met by laughter in some quarters and disapproving grimaces in others.

Many years later, the disapproving grimaces would materialise in other contexts where my view on "separation" did not embrace a concept of the church retreating into exclusive ghettos of isolation from the world. I have always believed that there cannot be impact without contact and bridges are always better than barricades.

On the Mount of Transfiguration Peter wanted to *"build three booths"* for Jesus, Moses and Elijah presumably to in some way "bottle the blessing" they were receiving. Had he done so they would undoubtedly have become shrines in the first instance and tourist attractions subsequently. He was not aware that at the foot of the mountain a demon possessed boy was waiting for a deliverance that would not have happened had Peter's plan been successful.

Over the years I have been asked my opinion as to what constitutes a 'spiritual person' and a 'spiritual church'. My answer has always been the same – those who are able to take the blessing from where it is to where it isn't.

Elim Bible College

A failure to do this turns the gathered congregation into incestuous blessing boxes where 'what we are receiving' becomes the core objective rather than what we have to contribute and to minister to the community.

Some years ago when visiting a church, the pastor having introduced me suggested to his congregation that they share publicly why they had joined the church. The various responses usually began with "before I came to this church…" and were followed with statements such as "I was broken" or "friendless" or "without direction" or "with no awareness of God".

To begin with this all sounded great, after all our founders named the Movement after an oasis where people discovered refreshment and shelter. However, I eventually developed a sense of unease. The first Elim was not meant to be a destination but rather a venue where they were resourced in order to continue on their journey. It seemed that this congregation perceived personal fulfilment, as important as that is, as a destination rather than a route.

Blessing for its own sake is not the Promised Land. Healing and restoration is meant to bring about the means of more effectively reaching out to others with the good news that the Bible calls the Gospel.

At another point in this book I will refer to those occasions when I have received criticism for engaging with groups whose theology did not precisely parallel with my own and interfacing with the unsaved. The Lord Jesus was criticised for the same thing. Those that Christ criticised the most were the Pharisees – the ultra-religious sectarian zealots who insisted that others conformed to their man-made rules and regulations.

A Harvard professor asked a group of his non-Christian, senior faculty for adjectives that they felt described Jesus. The list included words such as compassionate, generous, gracious, liberating and forgiving.

He then asked them for adjectives that they felt described the church and the words they suggested were – judgemental, bigoted, self-righteous, censorious, finger wagging and exclusive.

This dichotomy has to be bridged if the church is to be a people of influence.

****

Towards the end of my second year at college everyone who had successfully applied to be what was then called 'a probationary minister' knew that it would not be too long before they would hear about the church to which they had been allocated.

The procedure in those days was that the National Leadership Team (NLT), conducted stationing without any consultation whatever with the student concerned. Subsequently, and especially post ordination, the views of the candidate were considered – at that time, however, neither the minister nor the church were allowed to meet one another for interview before the appointment was made. But more of that later.

When the fateful day arrived a line of around twenty students gathered in alphabetical order outside the library to find out where they would be stationed. When my turn arrived I was summoned in and, on opening the door, I immediately recognised the two figures who sat at the end of the long table alluded to in an earlier chapter. One was the General Superintendent. On being asked to sit I was then handed a sealed envelope and asked to open it and read the contents before matters proceeded further.

I learned that I had been stationed to the small town of Llantrisant and was asked if I knew where that was. I replied that I assumed it was somewhere in Wales. This having been confirmed I was then asked if I was willing to take up the appointment. It was a rhetorical question for, had I answered in the negative, my ministry within Elim would have concluded before it had begun.

4

Llantrisant

Llantrisant is a small town ten miles from Cardiff. The church had been in the Assemblies of God but had recently applied to come into Elim. As I have said, in those days there were no interviews prior to appointment whatever the size of the church. The potential pastor was given the statistics of the church and the church leaders were given the name and a brief profile of the minister. Either could decline at that point if they wished to. It seems remarkable by today's standards but it was considered unspiritual to visit the potential town, and especially to look at the church manse if it had one, before making any decision.

The statistics for my first church were twenty people and £17 per week offerings. My salary, the only income I received from any source, was £8 and ten shillings (£8.50) which, while extremely small, bought far more then than it could today.

The church could not provide any accommodation, however, Ray and Anne Hughes, who were friends of my parents, pastored just six miles away in Pontypridd and they very graciously invited me to stay with them for a few months until I could secure somewhere to stay in the area. They remained lifelong friends.

Eventually I found lodgings with a retired couple. They were not Christians but often mentioned hearing the famous Welsh preacher Dr Martyn Lloyd-Jones on occasions in the past.

Some months into this arrangement we were having Sunday lunch together and they asked what subject I had preached on that morning. I said that I had spoken on the subject of grace. When they inquired further I explained that everyone had sinned and consequently could not attain heaven simply by the good that they had done. We were all therefore dependant on God's grace to receive salvation.

"You are not for one moment suggesting that people like us are sinners are you?" the lady of the house retorted. I responded to the effect that from God's perspective we all were sinners. The conversation lapsed into a stony silence and at the end of my meal I retired to my room. In the middle of the afternoon, presumably after they had been in discussion for some time, I was invited into the lounge and told that unless I apologised for saying that they could, by any stretch of the imagination, be categorised as sinners I would need to leave by the end of the month.

I was now in a difficulty as no other lodgings in the small town were available and the only recourse I was left with was to live in the church itself. It was a typical Welsh chapel surrounded by a balcony. In the basement was a minor hall, a small kitchen and an even smaller room which I used as a study. The furniture in this room consisted of a desk, a chair and Victorian style *chaise-longue* that I figured could just possibly accommodate a sleeping bag each night and that I could make my meals in the kitchen.

As the closing month in my lodgings drew to an end I considered what I might buy my hosts as a gift for being there. Knowing that Dr Martyn Lloyd-Jones was often spoken of as a favourite I purchased one of his books. I happened to know that this particular volume contained a chapter on grace. I wrote a short message in the front of the book expressing my appreciation of their opening their home to me and wishing them every blessing for the future.

I was not, however, destined for the room in the church as an elderly lady in the congregation, having heard what I intended to do, kindly offered me the spare bedroom in her tiny terraced house.

On the morning of my departure I handed the couple my small gift and ascended the stairs to retrieve my suitcase. By the time I returned to the hallway however, it was clear that they had read the inscription. The lady was in tears and both asked if I would consider remaining with them.

I explained that as I had now secured accommodation somewhere else, and did not want to offend my new landlady, I would decline but expressed delight that we were parting on the best of terms and as friends.

The son of Mrs Richards, my new landlady, was an elder at our church. He and his wife Margaret had two sons the older of which was thirteen and had asked his father for a guitar for his impending Christmas present. Knowing that I played the guitar his father asked me if, when I was next in Cardiff, I would look out the best guitar for the sum of money he wanted to spend. I, of course, was happy to do so.

The son was delighted and over the next few weeks I taught him a few chords. He quickly became proficient and after a Sunday morning service asked if I would listen to a song he had composed. Musically it was great, but I suggested that a section of the lyrics might be misunderstood and that he might consider re-writing the short section.

His graciousness, maturity at that age and willingness to learn greatly impressed me and I had a sense that with such an attitude the Lord would be likely to use him greatly in the future. I had no idea whatever that he would one day become one of the most important Christian songwriters in the UK or that he would lead a worship concert in a German football stadium attended by tens of thousands of people. Noel Richards and his wife, Tricia, went on to write several classics such as *You Laid Aside Your Majesty* and *All Heaven Declares.*

If there is one thing that I have learned in ministry it is that history moves on small hinges. Large oak doors that could not be carried by an individual swing effortlessly on hinges weighing less than an ounce. Small acts of obedience have opened huge doors of opportunity and small acts of disobedience possess the propensity to close large portals of possible potential. I believe that that Sunday morning was one such hinge for Noel. When God recognises that we are faithful in the little things he trusts us with possibilities exponentially larger.

My years in Llantrisant were extremely happy. I had taken on the pastorate at just twenty-one years of age and consequently the majority of those who were joining the church were also around that age.

One incident during my five year tenure stood out beyond all others. Llantrisant like most small towns, Welsh or not, tend to be sleepy places. Late one evening I was working on a message the subject of which was *"Narrow is the way that leads to eternal life and few there be that find it."*

How, I wondered, could I get this message over not just to my church but to the town that needed to understand it yet would not be present to hear it?

Our church building was on a hill so steep that the local single decker bus had to enter its lowest gears to negotiate it and its passengers to the top. What if I posted a sign outside our building large enough for everyone to read that would be unmissable? Everyone on the bus would get the message and the rest of the town as well given the church was on the main road.

The text alone, I concluded, would not suffice. I must construct a title that would leave people in no doubt whatever about the content I wished to convey. I also knew that, though it was now past midnight, if I did not post the order to the sign writer before I retired for the night I may not have the courage to do it the following day. The letter was posted.

I was to be away speaking at my father's church the next weekend, so this gave ample time for the order to be completed and I would paste the poster outside the building myself.

Before leaving for Manchester I stood back and surveyed my work. Here before me on an eight foot by three foot base, with black letters on an orange *Day-Glo* background were the words advertising my subject for the following week: *Why the majority of people in Llantrisant will go to hell.*

The following Sunday I was just about to leave my parents' house for the church next door when the telephone rang. The person on the other end asked if they could speak to Pastor Glass. Obviously assuming that the call was for my father I explained that he was not available but asked if I could take a message. "It's Pastor John Glass I am trying to get hold of and this is the *Daily Express* (a national newspaper in the UK)," the caller said. Was I aware of the stir that the sign outside my church had caused? The story, I was told, was already on the front page of Llantrisant's local paper.

I later learnt that there was a petition in the local newsagents that called for my eviction from the town.

The reaction of the local churches was very telling. The minister of the nine hundred seater church across the road from mine, which on a Sunday had a congregation of just six people, told reporters that my action was "no way to fill a church".

One of the letters in another local paper was from an elder of the nearby Baptist congregation who said that this was the first time he could ever remember hearing any minister of any denomination preach on the subject of hell. He then went on to challenge anyone who called themselves a Christian to say which part of the statement I had made was not true.

A few weeks later I was visiting my grandfather who was then the minister of the Elim church in York when the telephone rang and on this occasion the call was not for me. My grandfather was on the phone for some time before returning to the room to say that the person on the other end wished to speak to me. I have to confess when he told me who it was I was in some trepidation as the phone was handed to me. It was one of my grandfather's closest friends, the pastor of one of Elim's largest churches and a member of the Executive Council (NLT) who later became the General Superintendent of Elim.

"Hello John, this is Ron Jones here. I was telling your grandfather that I have read about the stir you have caused in Llantrisant in the *Western Mail* that reaches us here in Bristol." The pause that followed must only have been a second or two long but it seemed like an eternity. "I have asked to speak to you because I wanted you to know how proud I am of you. Whether people believe what we believe or not, thousands more folk are thinking about their eternal destiny than would have done so had you not taken this course of action."

Affirmation also came from one of the Movement's leading evangelists, Alex Tee. I had not consulted the leaders of the local church before erecting the poster but there had been no complaint from any of them. Only one person in Elim expressed any sense of displeasure. I was still at this time a probationary minister and he was the one to whom I was firstly responsible. He was a great believer in 'Pentecost with dignity' and to his mind what I had done had not fallen into that category.

The response that mattered the most to me came many months later in the form of a letter written in spindly writing from an elderly man in North Wales.

He had not been able to get my address and the envelope had been redirected several times before it eventually reached me. He expressed that as a young man he had become a Christian and believed the Bible to be the word of God. He went on to say that he came from a working class background and had had only a basic education. To the church to which he belonged came a succession of ministers eminently more knowledgeable than himself who told him that the bible was full of myths, much of it could not be trusted, and he should discount anything in it that referred to the miraculous. He was especially told that no one believed in hell anymore and that he should dismiss any notion of it from his mind.

He was writing to thank me that, in these closing years of his life, he had come across a young minister who still believed the bible to be true. I kept that letter for a very long time.

Not everything that I did during my time in Llantrisant met with the approval of the Elders and most of the difficulties centred around the leadership's view of sanctification.

The first problem arose after I had visited the home of a young couple. The young lady was a Christian and a member of my church but her husband, who she persistently prayed for, was not. I only visited the home when her husband was there but shortly after opening the door he would politely excuse himself and go into another room.

Knowing that she desperately wanted me to make contact with him, on one occasion as he was leaving I asked him which football team he supported. When he said Cardiff City I asked him if I were to go to a match with him would he come to church on the following day with his wife. He agreed to do so.

Within two hours of the final whistle being blown, and only shortly after arriving home, I answered the doorbell to see one of my Elders standing there. He said that he had come on behalf of the others to ascertain whether it was true, and he sincerely hoped that it was not, that I had been at a football match.

It transpired that the wife of the man with whom I had been at the match was the niece of one of the other Elders and she had phoned him to say how well her husband and I had got on together. When it was clear that I was unashamedly unrepentant the Elder left, his parting shot being that I was too often 'rocking the boat'.

The fact that the young man concerned kept his word, came to church the following day and committed his life to Christ had clearly no effect on my Elders who were, I should add, in every other respect good hearted and excellent men.

I have long since been of the opinion that you can't make an omelette without breaking eggs and some boats, especially if they have been stuck in the harbour too long, need to be rocked.

But things were to get worse in the following Elders meeting when I found myself again on the agenda. This time it concerned my taking a busload of our young people to a youth event in Bristol. It was not the meeting itself but where I took the young people in the afternoon before the meeting that had caused the crisis. "I took them ice skating," I said. "What is the problem with that?"

"The problem with that, Pastor," came the angry retort from one of the leaders, "is that while you and our young people were going round in circles, worldly music was being played in the background. This, together with the fact that you refuse to insist that women wear hats in church, means that my wife and I have decided to leave the church while you are its pastor."

In almost fifty years in ministry the number of people who have left the church because they have had an issue with me does reach to double figures. Sadly though, they were to be the first.

Before he left this leader brought up another issue with me. On this occasion he would be right and I would be wrong as will be explained in the next chapter.

The Elder and his wife who left my congregation in Llantrisant were also upset about the way our Sunday night service was being conducted. This small but growing church was attracting young people, many of which were exceptionally talented. Forty years later my Sunday evening 'Gospel service' may well have been called 'seeker sensitive'.

The accusation being levelled at me on this occasion was summed up in his closing comment, "The only difference between our service and TV's *Sunday Night at the London Palladium* is that those taking part do not go round on a circular moving platform at the end."

What he was asking for was the use of spiritual gifts and the kind of format that I had designated should be part of what took place in the morning service, but which I considered at that time was not appropriate at night.

****

Ten miles away from me in Llantrisant was Cardiff City Temple, Elim's largest church in Wales at which some special services were being conducted. Those who know the City Temple would be aware that the seats are tiered as in a theatre. I was in my seat somewhere to the back of the church when coming towards me was a friend of mine from my days in Theological College, also now a minister. He was accompanied by a beautiful young lady who I assumed must be his girlfriend. It later transpired that I had concluded wrongly. She was someone who he had been to school with years ago and whom he had invited to the special series of meetings.

A few months later the youth group from my church took a youth meeting at a Baptist church in Ynyshir, a village in the Rhondda Valley some twelve miles from Llantrisant. When I shook hands with the youth leader after the service I recognised that she was the same young lady who had accompanied my friend, Maldwyn Jones, to the service in Cardiff.

At the next Elim Conference Maldwyn mentioned to me that this lady, Marilyn, had commented on an article about me in a local paper – though not in relation to the previously mentioned incident I should add. It was a feature on the number of young people now attending the Llantrisant church and carried the embarrassing legend above my photo, 'The minister in flared trousers'.

Maldwyn suggested I should phone Marilyn on my return from Conference. I had met my future wife who to this day has been an immeasurable support in our ministry together. Maldwyn went on to pastor some of our Movement's largest churches and in retirement became Elim's official historian.

I was ordained in 1973, was now married and felt that although I was happy in the church in Llantrisant, I should approach our Movement's administrative Headquarters for a move. I was now twenty-five years old and this was the only time I would put my name on the stationing list. Whenever my role changed in the future it would be by virtue of being approached by others.

My name was offered to the West Bromwich church in the West Midlands.

The Best is Yet to Come

5

West Bromwich

Because of the way that stationing in our Elim Movement was conducted then, the first time that the Elders and people at West Bromwich saw me was at my induction service and it was, of course, also the first time that I met them.

The first leaders meeting took place within days of my induction and commenced with the secretary reading the minutes of the previous meeting. Apparently one of the Elders, being new to the role, did not know how the Elim system worked and, when my name was put forward asked the understandable question, "Do we accept the first name that Elim puts to us or do we have a choice?"

Sadly, the minutes could have been worded better for, with me sitting there, the secretary read, "The name of John Glass was put to the church and Cyril Evans asked, 'Do we have to have him?'"

There could not have been a more lovely and gracious man than Cyril and, after a moment of acute embarrassment on his part, the room dissolved in laughter and the group was quickly bonded.

They knew little about me and the only thing I knew about the church was that there were fifty people on a Sunday and that their offerings were fifty pounds per week.

What had not been communicated to me by Headquarters was that the church had a debt on the church building, the land on which the church was built and the manse in which Marilyn and I now lived.

In other words, our outgoings were twice our income. As a married man I was now earning £20 per week which was supplemented by Marilyn working part time as a tax consultant for a firm of accountants. I contacted Headquarters to say that, while I would not have necessarily declined to come to West Bromwich because of the accelerating debt, it would have been nice at least to know beforehand about the financial challenge it was facing.

The reply the General Superintendent of the day gave me was to the effect that he had been in the midst of a change of secretaries and that this data had inadvertently been omitted. He concluded by saying that he hoped I would enjoy my time there and that the Lord would "lead and guide me in the days that lay ahead"!

The other thing that had not been told me prior to my arrival was that an evangelistic crusade had been planned that could not be postponed because the advertising had already been printed.

The person conducting the outreach was David Woodfield who was then pastoring a large and growing church in Birmingham. I also later learned that, especially for a church of our size, a great deal of money had been spent on advertising.

Given the financial news that I had recently been appraised of, I hoped that the expenditure was going to be justified.

On the first night of the week-long event I was delighted to see how many non-Christians were present. My mood, however, was about to rapidly move to the other end of the spectrum within minutes of me introducing the speaker.

Given my firmly held position of making evangelistic meetings non-intimidating to the non-Christian, I was horrified to hear the evangelist say before he preached, "Let's all take some time to raise our hands and worship the Lord and if you want to 'sing in the spirit' please do so."

For those unfamiliar with Pentecostal forms of worship this means singing in tongues – a spiritual language mentioned in 1 Corinthians chapters 12-14.

At twenty-five years of age I did not feel it appropriate to express my concerns to someone who, though himself comparatively young, was several years older and certainly senior to me.

As this happened night after night I had a continual vision of our invested money cascading down a drain and was convinced that none of the people who raised their hands in the appeal would ever be seen again once the special services had ended.

I was wrong.

On the first Sunday morning after the crusade all the new converts were present and, as I visited them in their homes in the days that followed, the same story from different perspectives appeared time and time again.

In essence it went something like this, "When the evangelist spoke of Jesus being alive and relevant we thought, 'Well that's what he must be paid to say'.

"However, when we looked around the congregation and saw people like ourselves, that we regularly bump into at the supermarket, and saw them with hands raised and talking to God as if he was real, it was as if we were hearing one message from the front and many other messages all around us."

I also learned something else. When new converts attend their first 'normal Sunday service' after an evangelistic event it can be something of a culture shock. On this occasion, however, no explanations were necessary as the progress from crusade to the regular service was seamless.

A few months later I was invited back to my former church to speak at an anniversary weekend. The Elder and his wife who had left came back in order to hear me speak. I was quick at the end of the service to seek him out and to tell him that I now understood what he had been trying to tell me those years earlier and to thank him for the spiritual perception that he had had in those days and which I had lacked.

Sometimes we miss the truth of what people say because it is wrapped in the impression, real or imaginary, that they do not like us. Many problems in church life could be obviated by leaders and people alike understanding that when we reject what someone is doing we are not necessarily, by the same token, rejecting them.

I still hold to the fact that evangelistic programmes should be as cringe-free and accessible as possible. However, from that moment I never again believed that this includes censoring every expression of the Holy Spirit from the service.

Every church I have pastored, and every role I have occupied, has been in a context in which I have committed myself to be continually open to both learn and unlearn. It is the latter of those dispositions that so often challenges both our ego and our pride.

Unless individuals, churches and denominations are willing to engage with both sides of this coin they will never attain the status of what the bible refers to as 'flexible wine skins'.

This does not at all mean that we should jump on every passing band wagon, but it does require that we do not allow our strongly held convictions to become set in stone so that personal preferences become prejudices.

In my experience people who ride hobby horses generally want all of the road to themselves and, more often than not, appear willing to trample underfoot anyone who has the temerity to stand in their way.

When God told Jeremiah to go to the potter's house the prophet saw a vessel in process of being made that *"was marred in his hands"*. This problem was by no means insurmountable for, as the clay was soft and malleable, the potter was easily able to reshape it.

On a return visit, however, the vessel had been fired and was now hard. This time there was no remedy and the vessel was subsequently discarded as unusable. Remaining teachable and keeping our hearts soft is the key to all spiritual progress.

West Bromwich

Two huge lessons I learned while in West Bromwich took place during times of weakness and ill health.

The first expression of this was on a Sunday morning while Marilyn and I were having breakfast together before setting out for church. She was the first to notice that something was wrong as she sat at the table across from me. My face was becoming paralysed and within moments one eye would not close, I became unable to speak coherently or even to move food from one side of my mouth to the other. A doctor was called and I was taken to hospital with the assumption that, though only in my twenties, I had had a stroke.

I was familiar with Bell's palsy which was what this turned out to be. It is something that can affect someone for just a few weeks or for several months.

Because my condition involved a total paralysis of one side of my face I was told that I would not see even the slightest improvement for six weeks and that I would have to be prepared to be disfigured for the rest of my life.

I understood three things immediately.

The first was that I had been called to the ministry and the second was that it was impossible to fulfil my ministry in anything resembling this condition. The third thing followed logically from this. I would most definitely be healed.

By the Tuesday afternoon I was discharged from hospital as they could do nothing for me.

It was almost impossible for anyone to understand what I was saying as one side of my face was still completely paralysed and I had a black patch over one eye as it would not close.

That evening I slipped into the back of our regular prayer meeting but left soon afterwards as I could see that my condition was causing a measure of distress to some who were there.

When the Elders came to visit me the following day their obvious question was in regard to who would preach at the meeting on the following Sunday.

I had already prepared my message for that weekend and ironically it was on the subject of Divine Healing. I said that I would preach. They understandably recoiled at this as, given that they could hardly understand what I was saying in my home, why would I want to put myself through an attempt to preach at church? I remained insistent and said that I would speak for no more than ten minutes.

I did speak with some difficulty and when concluding asked how many required prayer for healing. When this had been indicated I asked those in the congregation seated near those who had raised their hands to pray for them.

I was still by the lectern at this point and looked out to see if everyone who had raised their hand was now being prayed for.

There was just one person had who no one with her. She was a paralysed woman in a wheelchair and had not been noticed as she was at the back of the church.

The paralysed preacher who had spoken on Divine Healing then went to pray with the paralysed woman.

The lady was not healed that morning but, as I prayed for her, I sensed something remarkable was happening to me.

When I got home I looked in the mirror and saw just the smallest glimmer of change. I had of course been told that there could be no change for six weeks and that I should expect to have some deformity for the rest of my life. Within six weeks, however, there was virtually no sign at all that I had ever been ill.

Knowing that I had been called to ministry when I was just a child, and realising that I could not fulfil ministry in the physical state I was in, meant as I said earlier that my healing was inevitable. I strongly believe that declaring something in faith that we know God has promised to us is the equivalent of walking on water. However, declaring something that we want, just because we want it, is the spiritual equivalent of skating on thin ice.

The second incident occurred some years later.

West Bromwich

I had booked a Dutch evangelist to minister in the church but the night before the meetings commenced I was admitted to casualty in great pain. A powerful painkilling injection was administered but within a couple of hours its effect had almost completely worn off. I pleaded with the sister on the ward for a further injection but this was denied on the grounds that I could either overdose or become dependent on the drug subsequently.

I could not understand what was happening. How could it be that a Pentecostal minister who believes in divine healing could find himself in a situation where he was pleading for drugs from someone who was not even a Christian?

I could see no purpose in what I was going through. I was serving the Lord to the best of my ability, I was not harbouring any known sin in my life, and the congregation I was leading had already doubled in size. What was the point?

I was about to find out and I felt the Lord speaking to me.

The fact was that I had been 'running the church' as if everything depended on me. I was even beginning to believe that the harder I worked the more results I would achieve.

I was about to learn a huge leadership lesson. Ministry is not about the minister, it is solely about the extension of God's Kingdom. Our 'success' is an irrelevance. God never promised to build my church he only promised to build his. I now became devastatingly aware that without his help I could not even take a single breath.

I was not in a maternity ward but something was being birthed in me that would remain with me for the rest of my ministry. This was not the first time that I would have to be humbled before I could learn something of importance and, as I shall share in a later chapter, it would not be the last.

Sometime later I would be given a book written four hundred years earlier called *The Providence of God*. The Puritan writer reminded me that God did not need any gifts, graces or leadership acumen that I possessed – though occasionally he may be willing to use them and, most importantly, when I was asleep at night, he could cope with the ordering of his universe without my assistance.

If I was to single out one further event during my time at West Bromwich it would be a point shortly after our financial situation had been stabilised.

Although our income as a church now matched our expenditure we still needed revenue to fulfil the vision that we had for the future.

I had been reading in my private devotions the verses in Proverbs 11:24-25 which say, *"One person gives freely, yet gains even more; another withholds unduly, but comes to poverty. A generous person will prosper; whoever refreshes others will be refreshed,"* and parallels with the words of Jesus in Luke 6:38 *"Give, and it will be given to you. A good measure, pressed down, shaken together and running over, will be poured into your lap. For with the measure you use, it will be measured to you."*

When our leaders next met I shared these verses with them and said that I felt the Lord wanted us to put them into practice as a church.

Elim churches tithe ten per cent of their offerings to the Movement centrally in order that national ministry, as well as local, can be fully resourced. What I felt we should now do was to give away a further ten per cent outside our church.

Two things became immediately clear.

The first was that, having just reached the point of financial balance after a period of struggle, this was going to involve a very real step of faith.

The second was that I could not expect our leaders to respond immediately without some time to think and pray about the matter. I suggested we should meet again in a week's time to make our corporate decision.

At the conclusion of the meeting my treasurer informed me that he and his wife would be on holiday the following week but that he would support whatever decision was reached by the leaders in his absence.

When we next met the decision was unanimous that we should take this step although some wondered how this would be received by the congregation when it was announced.

I have previously mentioned that the church was indebted in three directions, repayments on the church building we were in, the land on which it stood and a mortgage on the manse.

When my treasurer returned from holiday he immediately phoned me to tell me that he knew what decision the leadership had reached given what he had found in the post on his return.

It was a letter from the company who owned the land on which the church was built. They said that they had had a board meeting and, though our debt was not on their agenda it was inexplicably raised during their discussions. They were writing to say that they had decided to take the unprecedented step of cancelling our debt in its entirety.

The decision was taken at the very time that we had decided to implement Proverbs 11:24,25.

The following Sunday morning I announced to the church the decision the leaders had come to and, having let it sink in for a moment, then read the letter we had received subsequently from the owners of the land.

Five years after being in West Bromwich I received a letter from the General Superintendent inviting me to become the pastor of the Headquarters church in Cheltenham. I considered it a great honour to be asked, especially as I was only thirty years of age but, as Marilyn and I were happy in the church where we were. I wrote a letter declining the offer.

I had no sooner posted the letter than I realised I had made the mistake of not sufficiently praying about this but, through a set of circumstances that later transpired, the offer was put to me again and Marilyn and I eventually moved to our new church.

The Best is Yet to Come

6

Cheltenham

The Cheltenham church was unusual in that, by virtue of being next door to the Movement's Headquarters, thirty members of the congregation were either pastors or the family of pastors – including the General Superintendent, Field Superintendent, International Missions Director and National Youth Director. My colleagues in ministry often assumed that this would be an intimidating situation to be in but that was never the case. Without exception these national leaders could not have been more supportive.

The church had been pastored to this point by my very good friend Lionel Currie. We had been in college together in 1968. Apart from being an exceptional pastor he was, and still is, one of the finest bible teachers our Movement has ever produced and, had he and his wife Ruth not given nine years of their life to minister in Ghana, would, I'm sure, have occupied some of the highest levels of leadership in Elim.

The church was already full to capacity when I arrived so it was necessary to create space. This was done in two ways. David Ayling, who was then the International Missions Director and, incidentally, one of the three most godly men I ever knew, had been planting a branch church in a nearby housing estate. It was decided that a number of families move to this new church which they did. Before long, however, we were again back to full capacity.

The early 1980s were a time of 'stirring' within the Movement as a whole and a number of things were taking place simultaneously.

The Charismatic movement was emerging not just in the UK but around the world. These were churches from the historic denominations that were embracing a Pentecostal theology and practice while remaining within their own networks.

Parallel with this was the formation of what were then called 'House Churches'. This group emphasised relationship over structure, plurality of leadership and a much more informal style of service.

Elim at that time fell into two categories. The first were those who adopted a traditional perspective and considered any move in this new direction a retrograde step. The second group were considered radical in outlook. These were mostly young leaders but not exclusively so.

This latter group was itself divided into two camps. The smaller section wanted change and was openly critical of Elim's current leadership. The other, and much larger section, recognised that there was something that could be learned from the new churches that were emerging but saw no need to leave the denomination that they were committed to.

It was this latter group that I identified with. During that period I was greatly influenced by two publications. One was *New Wine* that emanated from the USA (not to be confused with the more recent group that bears that name) and *Fullness* published in the UK.

I was never for a moment tempted to leave Elim. This was not because I did not believe the new churches were unpacking a dimension of church that needed to be embraced but because of the derogatory way in which denominations were so often referred to on their public platforms and in private conversation.

I, together with many other young leaders at that time, saw this as incompatible with their teaching on relationship. For example, at one Bible Week the speaker encouraged those present to leave the *'valley of dry bones'* where they were worshipping and join a 'living' body.

Having said that there are two things that should be added.

I wondered if seventy years earlier when Elim was being formed and growing, not just by the addition of converts but also by transfer growth, our attitude then was any better than that of these emerging churches? I would like to think that it was, but a spirit of triumphalism may not have been universally absent from the way early classical Pentecostals conducted themselves.

Secondly, in later years some of the leaders of the 'new churches' have had the grace to acknowledge that things could have been conducted better and they should very much be commended for that.

As it turned out, the number of leaders lost to our Movement at that time could be counted on the fingers of one hand and this was due to three factors: the grace of God, a remarkable special conference held in Southport to discuss the issues, and the wise leadership of the then General Superintendent, Tom Walker, who acted like a firm and dependable anchor at a time when the ecclesiastical seas were potentially precarious.

I had been in the Cheltenham church less than three years when I was asked if I would consider becoming the pastor of the City Temple in Bristol, one of the Movement's largest congregations in those days.

The Best is Yet to Come

7

Bristol

There was a problem with any move to Bristol City Temple, however, in that the current minister, Jim Dick, one of my closest friends throughout my years in ministry, had experienced severe difficulties in the church which were not of his own making.

Jim's teaching and fine leadership was bringing a freshness and vitality into what was then a very traditional church. Some of those in leadership, who were against him, had suggested that if he wanted to take the church in this new direction that he should leave the 'state of the art' building in which they were worshipping and set up with the small handful of people who were likely to follow him.

The vacancy had arisen because Jim had indicated that, rather than do that, he would leave the church and take a break from ministry for a few months. He also strongly advised me that I should not proceed to the interview stage with the Bristol church leadership as, given that our philosophy of ministry was identical, I would encounter the same level of resistance that he had experienced, and Jim did not want Marilyn and I to go through what he and Margery had experienced.

Only a few years earlier, when in West Bromwich, I had made the mistake of looking at circumstances and drawing conclusions from them without much prayer. I was determined not to make that mistake again.

On that occasion I had initially not wanted to move because things were going well. Now I was not going to necessarily resist a move because there were potentially challenges ahead.

Having prayed I was totally and unreservedly convinced that our future lay in Bristol. However, the interview with the local leaders could not take place for a month due to the fact that both they and I had commitments that we could not re-schedule. I was not perturbed by the delay as I was convinced that I had heard from God and Bristol was our destination.

Early in the morning, two days before the interview was to take place, the phone rang and instinctively I sensed before picking up the handset that there was a problem.

There certainly was.

I was informed that the move was off as Jim had decided that he would be commencing a new church with what he anticipated would be around thirty people. This included some of the leaders who were sympathetic to the direction he wanted to take the church.

In the event, one hundred and forty people were present with Jim on his first Sunday. This meant that, were I to go to the City Temple, there would be no ground base of support for me. However, as the phone conversation continued, it was made very clear that Elim did not see this as an option as the founding minister was coming out of retirement to pastor the church and so there was effectively now no longer any vacancy.

I was now completely confused as I had been totally convinced that my next step in ministry was to be Bristol. I went so far as to say to Marilyn that I would find it hard to preach on guidance again with any confidence given that I had apparently got things so wrong when it came to my own ability to hear from God.

A few days later I was expressing my frustration to God in prayer when the phone rang. It was Jim. He said that God had told him that he was to invite me to come and minister alongside him in the new church. There was a problem though in that there was only enough money available to cover his salary and the hire of the school where they were meeting.

He went on to say however, that he was so convinced that God had spoken that, were I to accept, he was sure that by the time I arrived, the finances would be in place to meet the cost of my appointment.

Marilyn and I agreed that we should trust God for that and, when we were inducted into the church a few weeks later, the finances had risen to far more than just the covering of our salary.

Jim, typically gracious and magnanimous, now wanted to do something innovative in that both of us would have equal status. I felt this impractical as he was eight years older than I was, a member of the Executive Council (NLT) and was the pastor of the Bristol church long before the new church had commenced. We tried to model this innovative concept but I am not sure the degree to which we succeeded.

I learned a great deal during the time I worked alongside Jim. Jim and Margery were consistent visible models of the kind of church they aspired to lead.

Within a short time of the new congregation being organised we both realised that it was important to put a biblical structure into the church.

The people were with us because they hungered for a new kind of church unhampered by the religious stiffness that often accompanies dogmatic traditionalism. However, a desire for spiritual 'freshness' was not enough. It was now time to define what our vision and values were. Also, a group of leaders had come out of the original church with us, some of whom were deacons and some elders and we needed to define not just who should occupy those roles but what those roles meant biblically.

A desire for change was not enough.

There had to be a willingness to transition, learn and unlearn – and this needed to be done with maturity. Jim and I did not just want to be a 'different kind of church' we wanted to model how to bring change about in a biblical way.

We announced to the church that we would be going away for a number of days to think and pray. We rented an apartment in Bournemouth and spent much of our time walking on the beach as we talked the issues through.

We were especially focussed on who should be the leaders that would work alongside us. We knew that some who were currently designated Elders may need to step aside from the role and others needed to be invited to join us in leadership.

At the end of our time away Jim and I were sure that we had clearly heard from God about the way forward. What we were not going to do, however, was to make an 'announcement' to the church about what we were hearing from God – descending on the congregation like Moses from Sinai and expecting the church to receive what we were saying 'just because we were their pastors'. They were amazing people and deserved better than that.

We had seen the chaos and pain brought about by some in the house church movement through what had become known as 'heavy shepherding' and we were not going to go along that disastrous path.

However, when we came to church on the following Sunday the folk were anxious to know what would happen next.

Bristol

We said that over the next six weeks I would preach in the midweek meeting, which was as well attended as the two Sunday services, about the nature of the church, spiritual authority and biblical discipleship. When that was concluded we would ask the people if they wanted to walk with us into the vision we were going to outline.

Six weeks later the vote was unanimous.

I have always been grateful to God in every church I have pastored for the quality of leaders who have ministered alongside me. The leaders in Bristol were exceptional. One couple, Paul Clark and his wife Eileen, became lifelong friends of Marilyn and I. Paul was the greatest encourager and affirmer of people I have ever encountered in ministry. This tall, handsome man, who was rarely seen without a smile, had three degenerative diseases and was in constant pain, but never once did I hear him grumble.

Each year the four of us would spend a week of our holidays together. I knew instinctively when he was becoming tired or weak and would adjust the pace of the day accordingly.

One day, when he clearly needed to rest, Paul and I stayed in as Marilyn and Eileen went for a walk. Though we had committed not to talk about church business while we were away the conversation eventually veered towards the youth section of the church. There was a vacancy for a leader and we were thinking who might be a suitable candidate.

We verbally catalogued the gifts, talents and perceived 'coolness' of potential leaders. It was then that Paul said one of the simplest statements about leadership I had heard, "John, what our young people really want is not someone who is gifted and cool – they want someone who will love and care for them."

I am often asked by young leaders what I consider to be the three greatest attributes of leadership and I have no problem in enumerating them:

1. Relationship

2. Relationship

3. Relationship

I usually append to that the following story.

We were in a regular Sunday morning service when a young man gave a 'prophecy'. There was no doubt that in the past we had heard from God through his prophetic gift, but of late I noticed that what he was sharing fell short of the level of revelation that we expected and at this meeting what he brought was a case in point.

The bible requires us to 'weigh' prophecy for content. Leadership has a responsibility to guard the use of spiritual gifts. When there is too much money in the economy the value of the currency diminishes. When there are too many 'words' given in a local church the value and veracity of the gift similarly plummets.

Unless pastors are willing to keep the standard high few will listen to what is being said and even less will desire to operate in the gift themselves.

I approached the young man and, when I was sure no one was listening, I explained the problem as I saw it. I further asked him, irrespective of how strongly he felt the urge to do so, not to operate the gift for six weeks within which time he should seek God for a raising of the standard of the gift.

We were in a rented hall and time was at a premium so I had no opportunity to talk further. However, during the afternoon he phoned, with an attitude that I interpreted as being agitated, requiring to speak with me as soon as possible about what I had said. I arranged that we meet at the close of the service that evening. I assumed that he was upset by what I had conveyed and was of a mind to argue the point.

When we met he commenced by saying, "I have got one thing to say to you, Pastor." And then to my surprise he continued by saying, "Thank you for loving me enough to tell me the truth."

When the apostle Paul writes to the Ephesians about *'telling the truth in love'* he is not just speaking about how we select our vocabulary. He is talking about the context in which words, even hard words, are uttered.

Throughout this man's time in the church Jim and I had been quick to commend and affirm him whenever the situation demanded it if, for example, he went the second mile in serving others. He knew that we loved and respected him and we knew that such regard was reciprocated. In such a context of 'catching him doing something right' his ears were open to us when we suggested an area that may be able to be improved.

Two years into our time in Bristol on returning from a meeting of the leaders, Marilyn related to me something she felt that she had heard from God.

She said she felt God had spoken to her strongly that we were soon to leave the church and even the date, a few months hence, was specified. She went on to say that the Lord had also said that we would not move to another pastorate but that we would nevertheless serve Elim. She said that moments after this had been conveyed to her the doorbell had rung and on answering it found a woman she did not recognise who began by saying, "I am sorry to interrupt you but could I ask that, if ever you decide to sell your house, you might give me first refusal?"

This lady was not to purchase our house but Marilyn considered it a confirmatory affirmation of what the Lord had just told her.

I could hardly think of anything more implausible given that we were so happy in our current ministry. We could not wish for better fellow-leaders and people. Once again, however, I remembered my presumptive mistake those years earlier, that God happily overruled, and I began to pray about the matter. I was, before long, convinced that Marilyn had heard from God.

I shared our decision with Jim and the Elders who were understandably taken aback and they also, understandably, questioned the incongruity of the decision.

If I was going to serve Elim in a ministry context but not as a pastor then, apart from being a missionary for which I was not gifted, what would I be doing? Why must we move by the date specified? Why not wait until we knew what our new role was and stay in the church until that juncture? How would we live without a salary after the deadline had been reached?

We could answer none of these questions.

The following Sunday we shared our decision with the church family. It was one of the hardest things I have ever done. At the close of the service an elderly West Indian lady who led the intercessory ministry in the church and who we loved greatly, said that the previous night she had had a dream. In the dream she saw Marilyn and I walking away from her carrying a suitcase. She called after us to inquire where we were going. She said that in the dream we had turned around with the words, "We do not know but the Lord is going to make it clear."

Two weeks later the Elim Conference took place at Butlins in Bognor Regis. I saw that our chalet was near that of the Field Superintendent John Smyth. We knew John and Mary well as they had been members of the Headquarters church in Cheltenham when I was the pastor. I walked over to him and handed him a letter that informed him, as I was required to do, that we were leaving Bristol.

Knowing how happy we were there he expressed surprise and told me that a significant church had just become available and asked would I be willing to consider it. I said I did not feel that the Lord wanted us to accept another pastorate at this juncture in our lives.

I did not say, nor was it conveyed in the letter, that we felt that in the future we would be 'serving Elim'.

"Do you realise," he said, "that this letter is effectively your resignation letter from the Elim Movement?"

The weeks went by and we were rapidly approaching the deadline date.

Around this time I was visiting Cheltenham to attend a meeting of the Publications Board of which I was a member. At the close of the meeting John Smyth asked if it had yet become clear what I would be doing given that the deadline we had set for leaving Bristol was imminent. I responded that we did not but that we were trusting God for the future.

"Well, John," he said. "The Executive Council have been away for a few days to pray about the direction our Movement should be taking. We have been looking at the possibility of dividing up the UK into a number of regions into which we will eventually place leaders. This, however, is a huge step and we do not feel able to make the transition all at once. We have decided to commence with one region as a test-case to see if the concept works. We have chosen Scotland because it is the weakest area numerically. The Executive Council (NLT) have requested me to ask you if you would consider serving Elim in this new role. It will, of course, require a vote of the pastors and laymen in Scotland."

I had never been to Scotland in my life, even on holiday. What were the chances, I wondered, of Scotland selecting a 36-year-old Englishman as Elim's first Regional Superintendent? Yet the words that John Smyth had used were identical to the words that Marilyn had heard in her kitchen in Bristol. Your next step will not be a church but you will 'serve Elim'.

I submitted my name for election and was told that the vote was 100 per cent. I had three votes during my nine-year tenure in Scotland and on no occasion did I have a single vote from either minister or laymen against me. This was not so much a reflection of me but of the amazing bond that grew between us and the people in Scotland who we still dearly love. There have been no times in our ministry that we enjoyed more than those very special years.

The deadline of leaving Bristol paralleled perfectly with our move to Scotland. However, I realised that though I had been elected and had the strongest of possible mandates, I had not received any indication of what was required of me. Neither was there any precedent to follow.

When I put this to John Smyth he asked what I believed were my priorities in the order that I saw them. I had already given this some thought so listed them in the following order: be a pastor to pastors, plant new churches and train local leadership.

He then responded with the most releasing words I have ever been given, "Go to Scotland and fulfil your ministry!"

8

Scotland

Within three days of being inducted to the role of Regional Superintendent for Scotland I attended a Presbytery meeting. These are no longer in operation, largely due to a decision that I made and which I will deal with later. Those who remember them are divided as to their value. A few saw them as important forums for conversation and debate and others, among which I was most certainly numbered, considered them to be as ineffectual as they were boring.

The meetings consisted of reports from the various departments, a financial report and general debate. They rarely differed from one quarter to the next apart from the statistics being different by small margins. There was usually no spiritual input beyond the opening and closing of prayer.

However, this pre-planned meeting, which took place in Greenock on the West Coast, afforded me the opportunity to meet with the pastors and leaders and take any questions about the new role that I had taken up.

The first question came from a laymen who was well known not just in Scotland but via his contributions at Elim's national Conference. He was considered to be recalcitrant and argumentative and, to a degree the reputation was sometimes deserved. However, as I got to know him over the years I found him to be a good hearted and generous man in very many respects.

His first question to the young Englishman probably thirty years his junior was, "Have you been sent from England to change us?" I uttered a silent and deeply theological prayer which could be summed up in the three words "God help me".

I responded by asking a question that I knew he would know the answer to, "How long has Elim been in Scotland?" "Seventy years," he quickly responded. "And," I continued, "if you added the largest attendance in every church together on any given Sunday what do you think that number might be?"

He clearly had no more idea than I had prior to asking that question of our Headquarters myself just a few weeks earlier.

"Well I am able to tell you," I went on. "That number comes to just seven hundred. Seven hundred people after seventy years." And then I added, "Whether I change things or not I think we must all be agreed that somebody needs to change something very soon."

He and I got on famously from that point on.

Most of the population of Scotland lives in the central belt. If we think of the UK as a body and Scotland as a head, the central belt would be the neck stretching from Greenock in the west to Edinburgh in the east. Strategically, the best place for Marilyn and I to live would be in the new town of Livingston around seventeen miles from Edinburgh.

We had not been in our small bungalow for more than a couple of weeks when I noticed in the street outside a man with a black bag going from door to door and talking to people. It appeared that the Jehovah's Witnesses were in our street.

For some reason the person concerned never reached our door but it prompted the idea in me that it was time for Marilyn and I to make contact with our neighbours.

The first thing we did was to print a letter for two hundred homes in the immediate area. I concluded there was little point having a burden for Scotland if we had no burden for the streets around us.

The letter did not introduce me as a Regional leader or even a pastor. In essence it said that we were John and Marilyn who had just moved into the area and, knowing how long it takes to get to know people, we wanted to introduce ourselves. We were Christians who believed in the power of prayer and, if anyone would like to drop round for coffee or a chat about anything they needed to pray about, or just to touch base, our home would be always open to them.

Two people contacted us immediately and within a few weeks both had become spirit-filled Christians. Thirty years later David and Margaret Carson are great friends and are currently part of the Elim Church in Corby.

One of my goals was church planting and I had no intention of conducting seminars on the subject. The best way forward as I saw it was to start church planting myself and, hopefully, lead by example. The obvious first option was now the town in which we were living.

The population at that time was around forty thousand but it already had a Pentecostal church which had grown at one point to seventy people but after a split was now down to around thirty. It belonged to our sister fellowship the Assemblies of God (AoG).

I want to pause at this juncture to make the most important point in the chapter. The way that a church is planted has a direct influence on its future capacity for growth, in the same way that a bad birth can affect both mother and child for a life time. Planting for the wrong reason, or in the wrong way, is like building a house after first introducing termites into the foundation. That structure may not fall today but it will most certainly fall at some point in its future.

My aim in my first church plant in Scotland was not just to model the exercise but, even more importantly, model the way it should be done.

I made an appointment to meet the AoG pastor who was then working bi-vocationally as an insurance collector. I explained to him what I had in mind and made the following commitments. The first was that I would plant five miles from his church and, secondly, should anyone come from his church to mine we would require them to return.

He received me warmly and as I left asked if I would come to his church to preach – a remarkable invitation to someone who has just said that he was planting a church in his town.

I took this as an expression of courtesy but within a few weeks he pressed me for a specific date and I later preached at his church.

At the close of the service he handed me a letter which he asked me to read when I got home. It said that he longed to see a strong Pentecostal presence in the town but felt that it was unlikely to happen though his ministry. He committed to bring his people to every meeting when we launched in the local theatre and to meet me for prayer every day while those meetings were on. He later sent a cheque for thirty pounds towards our advertising.

George Chambers is in heaven today and quite possibly nearer the throne of God than many will ever attain, whatever the positions that they hold or size of ministry that they lead.

We were a long way, however, from launching a church in the local theatre. Our core group, including Marilyn and myself was just eleven. We met weekly in a small room at the local library to pray. Days before we started in the theatre one of our number, who we all knew as Miss Black, told the following remarkable story.

Thirty years earlier, when Livingston was just a small village, the government sent a man called Brigadier Purchase to oversee the construction of the new town. His wife and Miss Black became friends. It transpired that his wife had been converted in a crusade conducted by Elim's founder George Jeffreys and the two ladies met weekly for prayer. In one of those meetings the Brigadier's wife felt that they should pray that, as her husband was overseeing the construction of the new town, one day an Elim church would be planted in the town.

That prayer, now three decades old, was about to be answered.

Twelve months later I asked Roy and Jackie Monks to become the pastor so that I could move on to the next church plant. Under their sacrificial ministry the church bought the land upon which the current church building now stands.

Sometime later I noticed the same man in my street I had seen many months earlier going from door to door and speaking with people. He had not called at our home on the first occasion but was now heading in my direction. Some years earlier I had written a booklet called *Ten Questions No Jehovah's Witness Can Answer* so I was absolutely ready for him when the bell rang. As I opened the door he commenced with one question I had not anticipated, "Good morning, sir, would you like to purchase some *Betterware* brushes?"

The Livingston church having been established, I then focussed on the coastal town of Saltcoats commencing with a group of just twelve people. Within a year it too had grown sufficiently to support its own pastor.

Two things should be understood at this point. The first is that given all of my responsibilities across the country as Regional Leader, I was only able to devote a part of every Sunday to church planting. The usual scenario would be that I would preach at an established Elim church in the morning and at the church plant in the afternoon. The second is that my role then was greatly different from that of a Regional Leader today who has far more churches to care for and a far wider geographical area to cover.

It transpired that our Headquarters in Cheltenham were not universally happy with what I was doing north of the border and in consequence I was summoned from Scotland to appear before the Executive Council.

The charge against me was that I had cancelled the Presbytery meetings alluded to earlier. I was still conducting quarterly meetings but they were for leadership input, fellowship and prayer. All other 'business' had been dispensed with.

When I was brought into the room I was told that whether I liked Presbytery meetings or not that was not the issue. They were a constitutional requirement and they could only be disbanded by a decision of conference.

The leaders of our Movement were, of course, absolutely right. I had acted precipitously.

However, the Regional experience, having been seen to work in Scotland, had been rolled out across the UK and, that having been done, a resolution was eventually brought to conference that Presbytery meetings be discontinued and that Regional meetings, similar to the model that we had instituted in Scotland, be put in their place throughout the country.

One day, I was visiting John Seaman the pastor of our church in Paisley. John and Michael Epton of Edinburgh were the two most senior figures in Scotland at that time and I was immeasurably grateful for their loyalty, friendship and support during all the years I was there.

On leaving John's house, his wife Vera, a gracious and gentle lady, asked where I planned to church plant next. I told her where I was thinking of and asked why she had asked. "It's just that as I was praying recently I saw six people from Perth who said to me 'We are looking for a shepherd' and I wondered what that might mean."

I have to admit that if some people told me that – it may not be something that I would instinctively act upon. But Vera was someone who I believed heard from God.

But what could I possibly do about it?

I decided to place a small advert in the *Perth Advertiser* for just one week (if these people were there then I concluded that God was well able to direct them to a single advert).

The advert said that Elim was planting churches throughout Scotland (by now I was not the only Elim minister planting churches in the nation) and if anyone would like further details please contact...

There was no response and I concluded that that may well be the end of the matter.

I was wrong.

Scotland

Six months later I received a telephone call from a lady who asked if this was the number of the person who had placed an advert in the *Perth Advertiser*. I confirmed that it was. She said that she and some friends had been part of a heavy shepherding movement and that they had suffered badly as a result. They had seen the advert but knew nothing about Elim and did not want, to use her words, "To jump out of the frying pan into the fire." However, the advert had been retained and they now felt that they wanted to make contact.

She concluded by saying, "We are six people in Perth looking for a shepherd."

I met with the group every week for some months as they had been greatly hurt by those past experiences. Sometime later they had moved to a position of spiritual health to the degree that we were now ready for the new church to 'go public'.

As a result meetings commenced in the Salutation Hotel in the centre of the city. Within a year the congregation was large enough to support its own minister and today also has a building of its own.

During that period I was indebted to George Cuthbertson who travelled with me to Perth every Sunday after he had been to his own church service to ensure that we had music.

The primary object of pioneering is to see new people come to Christ – not the relocation of the Kingdom by people migrating from other congregations. Inevitably people do come from other churches and want to stay and, if numbers alone is the criteria with the pioneer pastor, he or she will welcome them unreservedly. A principle I learned very early on about church planting was to pray for only those people to join us that God was wanting to give us.

If refugees from other churches come to join you they too often bring baggage and wrong attitudes with them. If they have fallen out with their minister and insist on joining your church they should be asked to reconcile, if at all possible, with their previous pastor first.

This is not just a matter of integrity, it also has to do with preserving the base that you are building from so that it is not polluted by a toxic spiritual cocktail. Those who ignore this kind of advice usually discover that hidden attitudes have a habit of seeping through before too long.

At one Sunday service in Perth I noticed a young couple who were in church for the first time. It seemed likely that they were Christians as they appeared to know the words of the worship songs that we were singing.

At the close of the service I enquired if they were visiting the area – Perth is a beautiful city and an ancient capital of Scotland. They told me that they lived in the area and were effusive about the meeting and particularly about my part in it to the degree that I became a little cautious. "This is the kind of church that we have been looking for all our lives," they told me. They then went on to say that they led the youth and children's work in their current church and would now put all their gifts at the disposal of the new Perth Elim church.

Digging deeper I discovered that they were an engaged couple who each rented a flat. In order to save money they were going to live in one of the flats, though not living as man and wife, until they were married. "The leaders of our current church have said that, whether we were sleeping together or not, the arrangement would not be a good testimony. You, I am sure," they said referring of course to me, "would be much more liberal and generous in your view."

My advice to them was that they should seek a meeting with their leaders, apologise for their attitude and express gratitude for those who had such a sensitive care for them both and the testimony of their church.

I, of course, never saw them again.

Sometimes such approaches have far more depth to them. This might take the form of someone relating that they were in a 'dead church' and were 'getting nothing either from the ministry or the fellowship'.

While not wanting to comment negatively on their current church, but at the same time accepting their word, my approach was always to ask such folk to imagine that they were a candle and their church were a block of ice. If they felt that their presence there was gradually melting the ice, it was likely that God wanted them to remain where they were. If on the other hand they felt that the ice was in danger of extinguishing their flame then it may well be time to move on to somewhere else.

Sometimes approaches came from folk whose view of guidance were decidedly odd. On one occasion, when a lady informed me that the Lord had told her she must leave her church and join mine, I asked her how that had come about.

She said that during the afternoon the Lord had told her to make herself a cup of tea. This was followed by a further prompting to have a biscuit. "What do you think I saw as soon as I opened the fridge door?" she asked. "The biscuit was a *Breakaway* and I took this as a confirmation I should leave my church and join yours."

I never saw her again after asking where she might have ended up if the fridge had revealed a *Mars* bar.

A primary emphasis that I had when being invited to take up the role of Regional Leader was that of a 'Pastor's Pastor'.

Long before Regionalisation was conceived it had been a subject on many minister's lips. The Movement's leadership in Cheltenham would have been more than willing to help any pastor were they asked to do so but there were a number of difficulties associated with that.

The first was that there were just a handful of them and there were hundreds of ministers located in churches from the north of Scotland to the southernmost tip of Cornwall.

Secondly, these men were perceived primarily as authority figures and people in whose hands the stationing of ministers, and therefore a minister's future, were held. A young pastor struggling in any area in his life, would be more than reticent to share his feelings with someone in such a position. In consequence a problem may not reach the senior leadership of the Movement until it had gone too far to be resolved. However, it had always been my view that 'A fence at the top of a cliff is better than an ambulance at the bottom.'

Much of my first year in Scotland, therefore, was about building relationships with our leaders. Probationary ministers, now called Ministers in Training, were seen monthly, pastors four times a year and retired ministers twice a year. Once again, I should make clear that this is not an attainable goal by current Regional Leaders as their responsibilities are much more far reaching – something that, as I shall cover later, was something I was directly responsible for.

This, together with the fact that Marilyn would regularly invite people to our home, did more than just cement friendships. It enabled me to understand with far more clarity the challenges and opportunities that my friends and colleagues were facing and so enabled me to pray and plan more intelligently for the future.

Very few people realise what a vast land mass Scotland is. I was travelling on average 800 miles per week ministering at churches, church planting and meeting with leaders. The distance from our southernmost church in the borders to our northernmost was 269 miles.

It was vital that some sense of cohesion was created and, apart from visiting leaders, or them visiting us, further facilities were put in place.

The first involved Regional meetings whose content was now entirely based around spiritual input and fellowship and which we augmented with a residential retreat every twelve months. Given that it was a 400 mile round trip for a pastor to take from Alness to Glasgow I ensured that every minister's petrol expenses were covered so that distance and cost was never an obstacle to attendance. This meant that most attendance at these meetings were at maximum level.

Secondly, I stipulated that when visiting a church I would take neither ministry gift nor travelling expenses from a church, something that I continued into my time as General Superintendent. This meant that no church, however small, need concern themselves about the cost involved by my being there. Larger churches who wanted to contribute could donate to our church planting programme if they wished to.

Finally, a monthly magazine that contained teaching, local news and matters for prayer was made available to all our leaders.

One problem not isolated to Scotland alone was that although ministers received training Elders did not. If a lay leader retired from office a new and usually younger person would take their place. The only benchmark that the new leader had to operate by was that which had been set by his or her predecessor. Sometimes that was an excellent standard to follow but sometimes it was not.

The only way to approach this was to set our own gold-standard and template. This would not concern itself with how an Elder functioned in their role as that was a matter for the local church. It addressed who a leader should be before God, his or her peers, those they led and those in authority around them.

A course was designed that laid out sixteen traits and qualities we wanted to see expressed in lay leadership in Scotland. This course was rolled out across the country under the title of *SALT* – Scottish Advanced Leadership Training. It was taught over several weeks and, by the time I concluded my role, with one exception, no leader in Scotland came into office in any church unless they had been through the course.

Many years later, when I became General Superintendent, these qualities formed the basis of a series of short videos entitled *Cappuccino Communications* and are available on *YouTube.*

Several of our pastors were bi-vocational and, while in one sense I am reticent to single out any individual above another, a typical example would be David Bell who served as an Elder in the Motherwell Church, headed the Religious Education department of a local secondary school and served as Elim's national youth director for Scotland.

A few miles from Motherwell was the town of Coatbridge. Prior to my arrival in Scotland the church had suffered a split that left only a handful of people in attendance. After a time it grew to around eighty and I began to think about who to put in leadership.

I concluded David would be the ideal person. But how could I possibly invite someone who was already so overstretched? Nevertheless I decided to talk to him and, when I did, he told me that only days earlier he had mentioned to a friend that he felt I was about to approach him and that, if this happened, he would accept.

No sooner had he agreed, however, than a scandal occurred which was nothing to do with anyone connected to Elim but had the effect of reducing the church to just two people. On top of this we discovered the building had been vandalised and even the central heating system rendered inoperative.

As David and I stood and surveyed the damage I naturally released David from the commitment he had made. He would have none of it, however, and he and his wife, Linda, gave up two weeks of their holiday to marshal a group of Elim young people in Scotland to redecorate the place after professionals had done the necessary electrical, plumbing and construction work.

As the church grew, he left his work as a teacher and still continues with his wonderful family to lead the fine congregation there.

This is just one example of the calibre of men and women in Scotland who worked so tenaciously and sacrificially to bring to pass the growth that eventually materialised. Another elder who cannot be omitted from this narrative is Jackie Clark of the Glasgow church who served for decades and remains to this day one of the finest lay leaders I have ever encountered.

* * * * * * * * * * * * * * *

Election to the Executive Council (NLT) of the Movement was different in those days to what it is today in that any ordained minister who had two seconders would find his name on the ballot paper.

The Conference, consisting of all ordained ministers and one lay representative from each church, then voted people in place according to the number of available vacancies.

Two results of this were that the list was far longer than it is today and those who were eventually elected had probably been on the list for several years. The only person to be elected the first time his name appeared on the ballot paper was Colin Dye, the senior minister of Kensington Temple – Elim's largest church. Colin and Amanda are numbered among our closest friends and Marilyn and I hold them in the highest regard.

When I was approached to let my name go forward I had to give it some thought for two reasons. The first was that I was still in my thirties and the second was that, if at some point in the future I came into that position, how would that affect my relationship pastorally with those I was seeking to serve in Scotland? Would I become the authority figure that previously militated against people sharing what they were going through with transparency and openness?

The pastors in Scotland disabused me of that second notion as over the years a bond had been created that was unlikely to affect the strength of relationship that already existed. Marilyn and I do not have children and over a period of time many of the younger leaders that were emerging in Scotland we began almost to regard as family. When they succeeded it felt as if one of our own sons or daughters had succeeded.

I agreed to let my name go forward and though I was not elected at that time I was elected on the following occasion. I was then 41 years old.

The results were read out in the general Conference and as I took in the announcement I felt a tap on my shoulder. A young pastor congratulated me on my appointment and told me that when he was ten years of age he had given his life to Christ at a meeting at which I was preaching. Stuart Blount currently serves on our

National Leadership Team and holds one of the most senior positions in our Movement.

9

Kilsyth Church of God

I had just been unanimously elected for a further four years as Regional Leader for Scotland when I was approached by an independent Pentecostal church in Scotland requesting advice.

Kilsyth Church of God was an unusual church in a number of ways. It was the oldest Pentecostal church in Scotland – and some would say in the UK – and never had a salaried pastor in its ninety year history. It was led on Brethren lines by a group of Elders.

Their New Year Convention attracted people from all over the country and the pattern was that they invited two visiting speakers each year. One was usually from Elim and the other from our sister fellowship the Assemblies of God.

On this occasion, however, they had invited two AoG speakers. One was Warwick Shenton the then leader of AoG and the other Paul Weaver, the person who would later succeed him in that role.

They had both sought God about the messages that they should bring with a desire to speak prophetically into the life of the church. It was such a powerful convention that when it concluded the church secretary, Stephen Tee, the brother of Elim's leading evangelist Alex Tee, called the church to a special business meeting with just one item on the agenda, "How can we as a church respond to the prophetic input that God has brought to us in these services?"

Two things had been highlighted.

Firstly, that the church by virtue of not being under the covering of a denomination had become separated from what God was currently doing in the UK. It was therefore advised that they look for a network to connect to.

Secondly, that while their system of leadership may have worked in the past, there was now a need for the church to look for a full time leader who would bring vision and direction.

The advice that was being sought from me was, given the church was close to both of the two main Pentecostal groups in the country, was it possible to join both Movements? The same question was also asked of the leadership of AoG.

There is a group of churches within Elim which consists of congregations that were not founded by us but who affiliated with us because they wanted to identify with our vision and values. They are called ECI churches (Elim Church Incorporated). Their buildings are not owned by Elim and they operate with a strong measure of self-determination which has both advantages and disadvantages.

The two largest ECI churches are Bridge Community Church in Leeds and the Metropolitan Tabernacle in Belfast. There are also many smaller ones.

Though probably not an ideal scenario, it was at least considered possible for Kilsyth to be part of that group while, at the same time, being part of another denomination. The Assemblies of God at that time had no such facility so progress could not be made.

The church were clear that they had heard from God and so decided on another route. They would invite either an Elim or an AoG minister to be their pastor and, that being done, they would connect with the denomination to which that pastor belonged.

I was asked to suggest names. Potentially it was not going to be an easy church to pastor as the church had never had an individual leader who brought direction. Their 'presiding elder' was always speaking on behalf of what was essentially a committee. Nothing could be further from either Elim or AoG culture.

Secondly, the church was not just run on Brethren lines organisationally, much of the Sunday ministry was brought by speakers drawn from outside, some of which were non-Pentecostal in theology. Thirdly, the Eldership included a number of high calibre businessmen who were all strong leaders in their own right – something that some pastors may find intimidating.

I suggested six names and the AoG suggested one.

The presiding elder at the time was the late John Stark who had assumed that office from Jim Gibson Senior who had been in office in the church as either deacon or Elder for over fifty years.

It was from John Stark that I received the phone call informing me that the Elders had met and decided not to invite any of the names I had suggested.

I responded by assuring him that all that mattered to us in Elim was that they were confident they had heard from God. I went on to say that the Assemblies of God was a great denomination and if we could help them in any way in the interim we would be glad to do so.

"Well, we do believe we have heard from God but we are not inviting an AoG minister to be our pastor either," he said. "All the Elders are of the opinion that the person to take us into the future is yourself."

I was completely taken aback and responded that while I was greatly honoured by the suggestion, given that I had just been elected for a further four years by the Region, I felt I had to graciously decline.

"Well, will you not pray about it?" I was asked.

Memories of my failure to pray those years back when in a similar situation in West Bromwich came to mind and I said that the following week, while I was away taking a series of meetings at the Ulster Temple in Belfast, I would use some of that time to consider the invitation.

On my return I wrote to say that I had felt no promoting to take up the pastorate of the church. They responded by letter to ask me to reconsider which I again declined.

Another approach was made in the form of a question as to how much time I gave to each of the churches that I was pioneering. I responding by saying, "Half my Sundays and one mid-week meeting."

I was then asked if I would therefore take leadership of the church, giving that half day on Sunday and a mid-week meeting, for a maximum of one year on the basis that they used that time to look for a leader who could be their pastor. In return they would make a substantial financial contribution to Elim's church planting programme.

This was agreed and I commenced leadership of the church on that basis.

However, during that year the Elders said they were still convinced I should occupy the position full time and were totally convinced that they had heard from God on the matter.

I began to seriously lose sleep. It was not that I was unwilling to leave a national role to go to a small town. It was simply that I saw the Elim leaders in Scotland as more than just colleagues. To leave them would be, as I said earlier, like leaving family.

Also, although the church was led by and consisted of many wonderful people, there was a vocal element that I knew were not only not Pentecostal in experience, but were antagonistic to Pentecostal doctrine and practice.

I was not just passionately Pentecostal but I also possessed a far more radical view of what church should look like than most. The last thing I wanted to do was to bring my wife and I into something that may end in a church split.

One morning in the early hours, and still unable to sleep, I was praying. "How could it be that I had written books on hearing the voice of God and yet was currently unable to feel any sense of direction?"

It was then that a remarkable thing happened. I sensed the Lord saying that it was not that I was unable to hear but that he had chosen not to speak. However, on a specific date I would hear prophetically through a third party.

I looked at my diary and saw that the date fell on the Easter weekend some weeks hence when I was booked to speak at Birmingham City Church (BCC). I was to speak on the Sunday and, on the Monday, there was a Regional gathering scheduled to which other churches in the area had been invited.

I told the Lord that I was willing to be obedient to whatever the prophetic message said but asked that the person delivering it should be someone to whom I was previously unknown. This was an almost impossible condition given that I was part of Elim's national leadership and would be speaking at a convention at Elim's largest church in Birmingham.

I was so sure that I had heard from God about this anticipated encounter that I publicly related the account to the church at Kilsyth and said that, on my return the Sunday after Easter, I would tell them what I had heard prophetically.

There was no prophetic message during the Sunday service in Birmingham.

When the Easter Monday service began I noticed that the place was packed to capacity with about 800 people present.

I mentioned to my good friend Gordon Neale, who as Regional Leader was convening the meeting, that I would be grateful if he would mention before I spoke that I would need to leave the meeting immediately at the close of the service as I had to drive back to Scotland for an appointment early the following day.

The meeting ended without anything resembling a prophetic word. I made my way from the platform to the exit hardly daring to think of what I was going to say to the Kilsyth church the following Sunday.

It was at that moment that a woman stepped out in front of me.

She said two things that, under normal circumstances, would have offended most preachers.

The first was, "I did not come to hear you speak. I have never heard of you before. I do not belong to Elim. I attend the convention at BCC every year whoever the preacher is."

Point one had been covered.

The next statement was, "I have not taken in a single word you preached tonight as, when you came onto the platform, the Lord told me that he had a word for you that was going to change the entire course of your life. When the leader of the meeting said that you were leaving immediately after the service, and seeing that the church is packed, I have been sitting through the service anxious in case I should miss you before you left."

I asked her what it was that she felt the Lord wanted me hear and she said, "I see you walking towards what looks like an expensive piece of porcelain. You seem about to take it in your hand but then move away. You continue to do this in a state of indecision. The word of the Lord is this. 'Take what is before you in both hands. It will not split. It will not break.'"

Point two, the issue of the split, had now also been covered.

I returned home that night and in the morning wrote a letter to the General Superintendent of the Movement, Wynne Lewis, resigning from my position as Regional Leader for Scotland. The following Sunday I announced my decision to the church in Kilsyth. Shortly after I was inducted as their pastor.

The church had a remarkable history. The town of just nine thousand people has justifiably been called the most revival-soaked place on the planet and the reason for this is covered in detail in an appendix at the end of the book.

I was to pastor the Church of God in Kilsyth for seven years. However, in order that I could become its minister the local constitution required that a congregational vote should be taken on my appointment. I was later told that 85 per cent had indicated support. I was later to find out, however, that the 15 per cent who voted against would not be a silent minority. They would make it very clear that not only did they object to the presence of pastoral authority but would do everything in their power to oppose any new vision or Pentecostal style of worship.

The Eldership were well aware of the challenges ahead and in the first leadership meeting I conducted offered to resign en bloc – not because they were against my appointment but so that, to use their words, "I would have a totally free hand" to lead without having to force anything through the filter of an Eldership.

Some pastors would leap at an offer like that in order to fashion the future more speedily for, as we will see in a later chapter, changing culture is absolutely essential to all progress, growth or development.

I also knew that everyone wanted 'change' but the change that they wanted was change in direction and growth levels. People usually want externalised change but they often tend to resent 'being changed' themselves.

I declined the offer of resignations in the knowledge that a 'heart to do it' was the main thing and, though we may need to take things somewhat slower, it was better to journey as a team into the new future than to be driven by dictatorship with all its accompanying potential pitfalls.

One goal throughout this book is to share the reality of the situations I faced in leadership throughout my ministry. I have refused to wear the rose-tinted glasses through which selective memory is filtered – where successes and triumphs are pinpointed but the things that could have been handled better become blurred through an author's convenient amnesia.

We still have several friends in Kilsyth, but I would be less than truthful if I did not admit to the fact that the church at that time was to prove the most difficult by far in my pastoral experience to that juncture.

Marilyn's perception of those days would not parallel identically with my own and Kilsyth was to prove a church she would eventually find the hardest she would ever have to leave. This may possibly be because I sought to shield her from many of the tensions and the anonymous letters that were posted by those who remained staunchly opposed to the new culture I was endeavouring to implement.

On reflection I think I must have lived a charmed life to that point. The number of difficult church meetings in the four churches I pastored in the past I could count on the fingers of one hand. In my many years as Regional leader I can bring to mind only two occasions when I had to speak strongly to any pastor. Given the fact that in the vote on my next tenure after those incidents took place no one in the secret ballot had voted against me, I concluded that there was no resentment on their part in the same way that there was no resentment on mine.

The acceptance of leadership from anything other than a committee or a congregational vote was a struggle for some. The church had been so dominated by a Brethren mentality that women were not allowed to speak at business meetings. If they had a point to make they were required to do so via their husbands and, if they were unmarried, they must do so through a member of the all-male Eldership.

Within the first year I moved the church meetings to one per annum but my attempt to get the constitution changed to allow women to speak for themselves was defeated. It was eventually passed on the second attempt twelve months later.

The building itself was a barrier to cultural change. When it was first erected it had a state-of-the-art design and was a great credit to the vision of those who constructed and financed it. The issue was not the design of the church from its exterior but the layout of the 'sanctuary' area.

It had a platform and a heavily curtained communion rail that separated the pastor from the people. On a Sunday morning the Elders would sit on high-backed chairs in front of the platform, facing the congregation throughout the service.

Physical remodelling was needed to parallel the remodelling of a spiritual culture and I spent time with one of the deacons who was an architect explaining what I was trying to achieve so that he could grasp the design I had in mind.

The plans were approved and we vacated the building for several weeks in order for the work to be completed. It was not until I saw the final result that I saw how accurately he had reflected what I had attempted to convey to him.

What he had created far exceeded my expectations.

Gone were the thrones around the communion table, the high platform and the communion rails. White walls together with creative minimalist lighting produced an atmosphere of freshness and clean lines. The blue carpeted floor in the main area rose in a series of steps to a platform without any barriers between leader and people – the centrepiece of which was a custom-made glass pulpit.

Marshall McLuhan may not have been entirely right when he wrote in his book *Understanding Media* in 1964 that "The medium is the message," but it contained a truth that many churches still fail to grasp.

Shoddy and poorly kept buildings, meetings that do not start on time and carelessly conducted services that do not connect to those present make a 'statement' long before any sermon is preached. The first-time visitor is quick to 'get the message' and understandably rarely returns.

I was really looking forward to the Sunday morning service on the first day that we were back in our new building. The place looked amazing.

I spoke that morning on Nehemiah. Having seen the gaps in the walls of Jerusalem he had set about constructing something physical that would reflect a new spiritual beginning for the people of God.

When I concluded, and before we took communion, my associate minister Steve Kempton suggested that we examine ourselves to see if God wished to remodel and repair broken areas in our lives.

I shall never forget what followed. People spontaneously began to come to the front, many of them kneeling on the brand-new carpeted steps of the open platform. Several of them were weeping. We had a sense that we were on 'holy ground' not because this was a 'sanctuary' but because we were a sanctuary. Spiritual restoration and renovation was taking place. The only adjective I could image to describe the moment was 'awesome'.

Two days later I received an anonymous letter complaining about the service.

Traditionally on a Sunday morning after a time of open worship we would 'Come around the Lord's Table and break bread'. However, before that took place I would often read the passage regarding communion found in 1 Corinthians 11. That morning, however, God had broken into the service and, though we had taken communion, this passage in Paul's epistle had not been read. In total amazement I read to myself again the anonymous letter that asked, "How could those present examine themselves given the scripture reading had been excluded from the service?"

The preaching had been forgotten and the prostrate and weeping congregation overlooked. All that had been noticed was the infringement of a religious tradition.

I have always been of the view that in most churches there is a small minority that will rejoice when the pastor leaves and another section that believe he, or she, is the best thing that has happened to the church. The larger body of the church are just good people who have been loyal and faithful to the last minister, are loyal and faithful to the present pastor and should he leave will be loyal and faithful to the next.

When a minister understands this he or she has begun to reach a place of maturity.

When people at the end of a service suggest he or she carries 'a special anointing from God' they do not allow themselves to be flattered for they know that there are those in the congregation who may have an opposite view. Similarly, when they are greeted with less than warmth they do not become depressed. They know that there are those present who are supportive of their ministry and the direction they are attempting to take the church.

Most suppose that the Apostle Paul's *'thorn in the flesh'* was his eyesight but such thorns also take the shape of flesh and blood.

On a number of occasions I attempted to address issues such as Pharisaism and religion in my preaching. However, after one Sunday morning message Marilyn commented on what I had just shared on our return home.

I trust Marilyn's perspective implicitly. She is always totally honest. I have been encouraged and blessed by her affirmation over the years but if she feels that I need to address something she is also sure to let me know that as well. That morning was a case in point.

"You do realise don't you that the vast majority of the church are behind the vision and direction that you are introducing?" she said. I replied that I did. "Well, if that is the case why do so many of your messages recently appear to be directed only at the back few rows? If you continue to do this those who are travelling with you on this important journey will fail to be fed."

She was right. I recalibrated my focus and moved from preaching to the sidings and continued on the main line. I was back on track.

Few things are a greater litmus test for culture than music.

Kilsyth Church of God was immeasurably blessed with both the number and the level of giftedness of its musicians. In the days when churches had soloists, quartets and choirs Kilsyth had all of these and the male quartets, such as the Ross Brothers, were in demand across Scotland and the Kingsway Singers featured in large venues such as the Royal Albert Hall in London.

The music on a Sunday when I became the pastor consisted of a grand piano on one side of the platform and a Hammond organ on the other.

Very occasionally a group based around the style of music that might be found on a Gaither album would play – the line up being grand piano, guitar, bass, Hawaiian guitar and percussion.

There was also a third, though much less used, combination which would equate with a contemporary praise band which was led by one of the younger leaders, David Fleming.

The church, as it was currently constituted, had those within it for whom each of these styles were its preference. I concluded that to dispense with the other musicians and impose my personal choice would neither be right nor fair.

I well remember Noel Richards relating a story of when he and his band were booked to play at a concert where the opening contributors were a Swedish youth choir. While waiting in the wings he confessed to feeling a sense of frustration with the older style and wanting this to be over so that his band could get on to the stage. He then spoke of a very real sense of rebuke that came from the Lord who said, "Noel, do you think I have a preferred style or do you think I am simply looking for a people who will worship me in spirit and in truth?"

In other words, if people have a style of music – be it medieval plainsong, classical, country and western or rock – that augments their sense of worship and connection with God who has the right, via their subjective preferences, to deny them such access?

With that in mind I introduced the idea of what I called 'Designer Worship' which in essence meant that the three musical styles in our church would rotate ensuring that, in a three week period, everyone would hear their preferred music. It also meant that everyone would have the opportunity to enjoy, and hopefully appreciate, the musical preferences of others.

It worked for a while.

Its demise occurred on a Sunday morning when the contemporary band were playing the newly written song by Darlene Zschech entitled *Shout To The Lord*. It was 1993 and the effect on the service was electrifying. The congregation was applauding the Lord and spontaneous shouts of praise were taking place all over the church.

Then it happened. Two young married couples rose very noticeably from the seats that they always occupied near the front. The men tucked their large black *Authorised Version* Bibles under their arms and very publicly stormed down the aisle to the back leaving no one who watched them in any doubt as to their disgust as to where they saw 'worship going' in the church.

From that moment 'Designer Worship', which was predicated on the proposition that when our preferred music style was not in place we would seek to appreciate the styles of others, came to an abrupt end.

The dissenters were from the groups that preferred the Gaither style of music. It was always assumed that I did not like this style of music. The truth is that I thought it had its place. What I did not like was the attitudes of those that liked it – which was something else entirely.

The man and woman who played the Hammond organ and the grand piano asked to see me. They said they did not have any problems with the 'new music' and in fact enjoyed and appreciated it. They felt that their style of music had reached the end of its journey and thought the contemporary worship style was the best way forward.

This meant that from that time onward the contemporary band became the regular leaders of worship.

These guys, led by Dave Fleming, were phenomenal musicians and spiritually sensitive. This band was a perpetual joy during the time I led the church and were in the forefront of the developing change of culture in the years that followed. I honestly believe that there was not a better worship team in Scotland in those days.

It's worth noting that in those turbulent times, none of the dissenting factions left the church. The prophecy that had brought me there in the first place had said, "Take it in both hands, it will not split and break."

As I have said previously I have always had a close affinity with our sister fellowship the Assemblies of God. During those days in Kilsyth a group under the leadership of an AoG minister, Peter Cochrane, thought it would be a good idea to conduct a Bible Week at the Butlins holiday camp in Ayr under the joint auspices of the main three Pentecostal denominations in Scotland – Elim, AoG and the Apostolic Churches. It was called *PLUS* - Pentecostals Linked United in Service. The two main speakers for the event were Warwick Shenton (AoG National Leader) and myself. It was decided that we would alternate on each of the morning and evening celebrations.

I knew that Warwick was to undergo an operation prior to this special event. He was a close friend and had emailed me just before going into the operating theatre. He was booked to speak in my church in Kilsyth on the following weekend.

I arrived at the Butlins holiday centre and within an hour two dramatic things took place. The first was that, as I went into the chalet in which I was to be accommodated, someone ran up to me and asked if I had "heard the news".

Warwick had unexpectedly died on the operating table.

I could not believe it. As the people who had brought the message left they added, "Of course you will now need to be the speaker at all the morning and evening celebrations. It's too late to book anyone else as we are starting tonight." I fulfilled all the engagements that week with the exception of one where Paul Scanlon (Bradford) spoke.

I received this news of Warwick's tragic death on one side of the threshold of the chalet but, as I went through the door, I felt the Lord say, "You also are about to be taken ill." It was now noon and the first meeting was to begin at 6:30pm.

By 4:30pm I began to feel very unwell indeed. I did not confide in anyone else as to how I was feeling as, given the announcement that had been made in the service about Warwick, I did not want the organisers to become unnecessarily anxious.

At around 3am in the morning I experienced the worst pain I have ever known in my life – and given that I had had kidney stones on two occasions in the past I certainly had a bench mark to measure pain by.

Kilsyth Church of God

I was in a room on my own and there was no one at that time of night I could contact. I struggled to my car and eventually found a hospital. No one could explain why I was so ill and I eventually got back to Butlins to face the rest of the week. Over the next six months I would end up in casualty on virtually every occasion I ministered away from home. No one, including private consultants, could diagnose what was wrong. Eventually an operation took place that removed a diseased gall bladder and the problem ended.

Despite what was going on behind the scenes, the conference was everything and more than the organisers had hoped for. The highlight for me was to see our praise band from Kilsyth seamlessly worshipping alongside musicians from an AoG church. I watched how the two main worship leaders deferred to one another. There was a total absence of ego on the platform. All these top musicians were operating under a single agenda – bringing people into the presence of God.

I have seen this synergy since – most poignantly in the formation of *Elim Sound* which I shall allude to in a later chapter – but this was the first time I had witnessed such a thing and I was immeasurably blessed by it.

****

It was during my time at Kilsyth that the church reached its centenary. It was a congregation before it became the first Pentecostal church in Scotland.

I invited three speakers to take part in this special event. One was the General Superintendent of Elim, Wynne Lewis, the other was Mike Sherwood who had been a close friend since our days in college in the 1960s. The third was Ken Gott.

Ken was a well-known speaker in the Assemblies of God and his church in Sunderland had experienced a particular revival that was manifested in meetings that took place every night of the week and which were attended by hundreds of people – many coming from various parts of the world to witness for themselves what was taking place. I spoke once a month at those remarkable meetings.

However this was not the reason why Ken and his lovely wife Lois were invited to the centenary. Ken's family had been members of the church from its earliest days.

Meeting Ken in the church car park on his arrival he immediately handed me a large format book. He explained that he had been one of the speakers at the Brownsville Revival in Pensacola, Florida, and he said that the senior minister, John Kilpatrick, had given him three copies. One was for himself, the other was for Lois' father who had been a prominent AoG minister and the other he said was for someone who the 'Lord would reveal to him should have it'.

The book was a church bulletin published as the revival had unfolded in Azusa Street in Los Angeles almost a hundred years previously. Ken said that, as Kilsyth was mentioned in the bulletin several times and this was our centenary, it was obvious that I was the person who should have the third copy. However, there was another factor in Ken's visit that would be significant.

The speaker on the previous day was Wynne Lewis and he had been staying in our home. The moment he stepped in the door he said that he had been asked by the Executive Council (NLT) of Elim to approach me to move from Kilsyth to take up a senior role in the Movement.

I told him that I was called to Kilsyth and I felt that this is where I should be until the Lord showed me otherwise.

Returning from the evening service Wynne again attempted to convince me it was time to move. This conversation continued the following morning before a driver took him to his next appointment and before I went off to the service at which Ken would be preaching.

Even as he got into the car he said, "It's time to move John, I will phone you at 8am tomorrow morning for your final answer." I assured him that he had already received my final answer but I would of course take his call.

Kilsyth Church of God

During Ken Gott's message, while not aware of the conversation I had had with Wynne a few hours earlier, he stopped addressing the church, and in front of the entire congregation, pointed at me and said, "God has entrusted something to you. Do not lay it down until God has said it should be laid down."

Wynne phoned the next day and, when I related the story, he graciously accepted the situation.

A year earlier, knowing that the centenary would be taking place, I had wanted to surprise the church with what I hoped would be a great means of marking our centenary.

I approached Scottish Television and suggested that as Kilsyth Church of God was the oldest Pentecostal church in Scotland, would they like to broadcast a Sunday service to mark this event at prime time.

When some months passed without even getting an acknowledgement of my letter I concluded that this was one surprise that was not going to materialise.

I was to be proved wrong.

Several months after my initial approach I received a call from the head of religious broadcasting. He related that in the process of removing a filing cabinet in his office his staff had found my unopened letter that had fallen between the furniture.

He said that he had to be honest and say that, had it arrived on his desk in the normal way, he would have sent a polite response declining my suggestion on the basis that the number of Pentecostal churches in Scotland was small in comparison with the membership of other denominations and that in the history of STV no Pentecostal service had ever been broadcast.

"However," he went on, "given that we have been remiss in not giving you the courtesy of an answer, I am willing to send a team to your venue to meet you and to see if the building is suitable for a broadcast. I must say though it is unlikely that we will be in a position to proceed."

The Best is Yet to Come

When the day arrived my secretary announced that they were here and, as I walked from my office to the main church area, the Lord clearly spoke to me and told me that the man who was leading the team and was the primary decision-maker was from the town of Sligo in Ireland.

I walked through the door and greeted the person who was clearly the leader and as he said, "Hello," I responded with, "So you are from the town of Sligo then?"

"How on earth would you know that?" he asked with a smile. "The only person who has ever recognised my accent was a woman I met who later became my wife. Did STV tell you where I was from or did you once live there?"

"Not at all," I said. "Though my family are from the north of Ireland I have been to the Republic only once and never to Sligo." And then added, "God told me."

A great rapport was established between us from that moment and he subsequently agreed not to one hour-long Sunday morning service but to three. They were to be pre-recorded over two evenings and huge lighting rigs were placed outside the church and shone into the windows to give the impression that the recordings had been made on a sunny Sunday morning.

A number of other remarkable things resulted from those three services.

At the close of one of several meetings that took place at the church before the recordings were made my new friend from STV, as he was about to leave my office, turned and said, "You know, John, when we do even a single broadcast the church consider it a great privilege and cannot do enough for us. This means we only have to say 'jump' and the only response they tend to make is 'how high?'

"I have never said this before in my career, but anything we can do for you we will and when you want us to jump it will be us who are asking 'how high?'"

The relationship we had was such that I felt I could joke with him by saying, "Oh, if that is the case then, during my preaching I will do what the TV evangelists in the States do and point directly to the main camera and address the audience personally."

I knew this concept was anathema to British broadcasters and I was not for a moment seriously considering it as an option.

To my absolute amazement he said, "John, if at any point you feel that is what you want to do – go for it."

I was later to take him at his word.

Shortly before the first recording of the first two back-to-back services I saw while praying two scenes. The first was of a grieving woman and the second of a young woman watching the programme on a settee accompanied by small children. It was clear that this woman was unwell and struggling as a single parent.

In the first service I pointed at the camera just momentarily as I preached. In the second service I did the same thing at another juncture in my message.

Months later I received a letter from a lady in Glasgow who had switched on the TV and while watching had seen me point to the camera while saying, "And you are sitting there on the settee with your children forsaken by the person who committed themselves to you in marriage and in the worst health you have ever been. Though others have let you down, Jesus promises never to leave you or forsake you."

This single parent had wrecked her body through substance abuse and did not know which way to turn. She later attended her local Elim church in Glasgow and turned her life over to Christ. She wrote to me to let me know how her life had changed and later recorded her testimony in her own words in *Direction* our Movement's national magazine.

One of my favourite Scottish preachers is Jay Fallon, a man who was once a heroin addict and who later headed up *Teen Challenge* in the UK. I had booked him to preach in Kilsyth and as he turned up at the church his face was radiant. As he entered the building he said, "John, I could not be more happy. This morning I dropped by to see my mother on the way to church and before I left was able to lead her to Christ. She has had no church background at all and so when I said as I left that I was off to speak at Kilsyth Church of God she amazed me by saying, 'John Glass is the minister of that church isn't he?'

"I asked her how on earth she would know that given that she did not know any other Christians apart from myself let alone ministers of churches.

"She said that a short time after she had walked in on her daughter's (my sister's) suicide she was totally distraught. She did not know anything about the morning service but turned the TV on and, as she did so, saw you point from the screen with the words, 'Though you have suffered the worst imaginable pain and bereavement, God is there – right where you are.'"

Though I have highlighted examples of some of the challenges of the church it would be wrong to create the impression that my entire time was a burden. In fact, as I have said previously, although Marilyn has enjoyed being part of all the churches at which I have pastored, Kilsyth was the hardest for her to leave when we eventually did so some years later.

One of the remarkable features of the church was the *Golden Days* meeting that took place every Thursday. Many pastors only speak about their youth culture events even though one of the greatest areas of potential in many churches is the involvement of the over sixties.

Golden Days was amazing and run by a team from within it that attracted around a hundred and forty people every week – some of which came from other churches in the town. It comprised of great music within its own genre and always provided phenomenal catering.

Some of the great characters in the church were from families that had been there for generations – the Andersons, the Grays and the Gibsons.

Jim Gibson Snr, as I said at the commencement of the chapter, had been a deacon, Elder and presiding Elder in the church for over fifty years before I arrived. When all the changes were taking place, and the dissenters were expressing everything between unhappiness and anger about the way the church was changing, it would have been very easy for him to act as a magnet for the malcontents. He refused to do so.

As I stood at his graveside many years later I thanked God for a man whose integrity matched his great gifting.

It was during my time in Kilsyth that I had one of the most remarkable spiritual encounters of my entire life.

Warwick Shenton, who I have referred to earlier, apart from being the leader of Assemblies of God in the UK, for a period also spoke regularly at a church in Salinas, California and gave this church apostolic covering. He visited there regularly and, when he was unable to fulfil one of his dates, the pastor asked if he could recommend someone to come across to take a week's meetings.

Although I was not in AoG Warwick for some reason recommended me.

Travelling in a packed economy class for fourteen hours is not something to be relished. I find it hard to sleep on a plane journey at the best of times and there were some points in the trip when I asked myself why on earth I had taken an appointment to a church that I knew nothing about.

When I arrived in San Francisco airport I was met by an elderly couple who said that they were the pastors and they took me to a small house on the grounds of their church which would be my base for the week's meetings.

When I arrived for the first service I could tell that this church was different from anything I had encountered before. The leaders' prayer time before the meeting was clearly not a formality. It was incredibly powerful.

The first thing that I noticed as the service began was the incongruity of the whole situation. On one hand everything was being 'done wrong' and on the other hand the church was packed to the doors with young married couples and their families who were totally engaged in the service.

I was later to learn that this church had been in revival for four years with meetings every night of the week all of which had maximum attendance.

So what was 'wrong'?

To begin with the worship was led by the elderly minister who bizarrely was leading the worship by waving his hands and conducting as if the church were in the 1950s. Secondly, the worship team were on the opposite end of the 'cool' spectrum and, although in California, were dressed like *The Waltons* – for those who remember the TV series of that name.

However, night after night, the presence of God was almost tangible. After each service I would return to my simple accommodation and go through the same routine. I would sit in the chair beside my bed trying to take in what had happened before eventually retiring for the night.

The series over the week that I was speaking on was *The Glory of God*. I had come with a sermon series but would be going away with a whole new sense of what the glory of God meant.

During one of the worship times I turned to the old pastor and said, "This is so amazing, I would sacrifice anything to constantly experience this level of anointing. How did this all begin?"

The so-called Toronto Blessing had begun in Canada but this church had heard nothing of it.

I anticipated several things that he might relate that could have become the catalyst for what was happening. I was staggered when he said, "No one in this church owns a television."

That evening when I phoned Marilyn to say how the meetings were going I told her, "We may be getting rid of our TV."

Before I left the pastor gave me a book to read on the plane home entitled *Ten Arguments Against Television*. I started it at the airport and what I read was a revelation. It talked about media inculcating a secular theology where the *'theos'* was the god of this world.

I began to think of some of the young people in my church back home who were not engaging at all with the things of the Spirit and were possibly only 'in church' because their parents made them attend. I realised the forty minutes in the week that they heard me preach had to offset the many hours of a secular world view that they were receiving from TV and the culture being fed to them in their schools and social connections.

I read statistics such as when in a TV soap one character said to the other, "Let's go to bed", 95 per cent of the time they would not be referring to their husband or wife.

It was clear that when young people were being bombarded with messages such as those that a call for purity – biblical norms sounded like something from the *Twilight Zone* and totally disconnected from a world where 'everyone was doing it' – the 'it' being translated into a myriad of secular cultural 'norms'.

Like most Christians I had controlled the TV by switching channels when I encountered something inappropriate. What I had not realised to that point was that, simply by just imbibing the apparently innocuous, I was taking its toxic effect into my spirit. It was as if I was drinking from a stream that did not appear polluted but had a degree of toxicity that over time was spiritually detrimental.

When I boarded the plane home I was told I had been upgraded to business class for the fourteen hour flight which meant that I was sitting alongside just one other passenger. After the initial introduction we both settled down to the reading matter we had brought with us for the flight – he to his book and me to mine. Mine was *Ten Arguments Against Television*.

As I continued to read I sensed him looking across to the spine of my book to read the title. I naturally have no problem in people seeing me reading a Christian book and on a few occasions have read my bible. I was, however, embarrassed as this young man in his thirties kept peering over to my book, the title of which I knew must appear ridiculous to him.

Eventually he asked me outright what I was reading. When I told him I was surprised by his response. He said that he was a newly qualified medical doctor who was about to be married. He was also a committed Christian. He said that he and his fiancée had made a commitment that in the first year of their marriage they would not have a TV in their home as they wanted to concentrate on their relationship rather than staring at a screen in the corner of a room for the entire evening when they were together.

He considered his meeting me as a confirmation of their decision. I considered that meeting him was evidence that God wanted to impact my ministry by decisions that I would soon make.

On my first Sunday back in Kilsyth I related the story of the amazing church I had been to. It was like returning home to your wife and enthusiastically talking about this wonderful woman that you had met with the implication, "If only you could be like her."

I announced to the church that I would be going on a three month TV fast in which I would not even watch the news. I assured them that I would not be insisting that they join me.

There is nothing worse than a pastor inflicting revelation on people who, were they to comply, would be doing so out of a loyalty that would quickly degenerate into the conformity of a religious duty should it not be a conviction that they felt they were personally receiving from God.

What I was not aware of was that my worship leader, David Fleming, was making a personal decision about such a fast – though for a shorter period.

What happened next was an unparalleled transformation of my ministry. Prayer took on a new dimension, I was ministering at a fresh level and I began to receive accurate words of knowledge for total strangers in restaurants and airport lounges. Given what David had done, the level of his worship leading went to a much higher strata than ever before.

When my TV fast ended, in the same way that people after a prolonged food fast can only take food in small amounts, I found it hard to watch TV for more than a few minutes at a time.

I want to make it clear that I am not advocating that Christians should remove TVs from their homes. We have TVs in our home today which I regularly watch.

What I am advocating is that Christians consider a media fast from either TV, social media or the internet. The best way might be to start with a week and progress to a month or more at a later point. It provides a powerful spiritual detox.

The story and impact of Salinas did not end there, however.

Two years later I was approached by the church in Salinas to say that an Elder and his wife from the church would be touring the UK with some of the young women from the church and would I like to have them in our church.

I could not think of anything I would like more. There was, however, a problem.

The only dates that were free came on a mid-week night after a two-week intensive evangelistic programme that most of the church had been involved in over several consecutive nights.

How could I suggest that they come out yet again for this unscheduled service?

They did however attend. I had gone on at such length about this church that even the most tired came simply out of curiosity.

Things were then to take an unexpected turn.

I had asked the Elder, a middle aged man, to minister and the young women to sing. The music was good but it was clear that the atmosphere in California was not being translated to Kilsyth.

The difficulty arose when the preacher got up to speak.

I was sitting on the front row and within minutes it was apparent that he was overwhelmed to the point of incoherency. He was beyond nervousness and glanced down at me on a couple of occasions with a look that said, "Please let this stop and get me out of this."

The Best is Yet to Come

I looked round at the congregation and saw scores of pairs of eyes looking right back at me as if to say, "Why have you brought us out to hear this? It is dreadful."

The attendance was amazing for a mid-week service and also in attendance were the young people about whom I remained so concerned as to their spiritual life – people who always appeared to wish they would far rather be out clubbing than being at church.

I looked back at the speaker and, as he was almost in a state of panic, I made my way to the platform and stood next to him.

Putting my arm around his shoulder I addressed the congregation and said, "Every speaker has moments when things go wrong, myself included, and this is obviously not a comfortable time for our guest this evening."

As I spoke I could sense the gratitude coming from him as I introduced this exit strategy.

As this was just about the worst meeting I had ever attended, I had in mind to close the meeting with prayer. But it was still only 8:15pm.

Thinking that this may be a little abrupt I suggested that the young women sing a final song before we closed. The song they chose I remembered from when I was at their church. The tune was a simple three-chord chorus and the lyrics predictable:

> *Fill me Jesus, Fill me now,*
> *Fill me Jesus with thy Holy Ghost and power.*
> *I am thine, O Lord, to do with as thou wilt,*
> *Fill me Jesus, Fill me now.*

What then happened was almost beyond belief.

The power of God hit the church. Right across the congregation the same people that moments earlier were frustrated with the meeting began to weep and to sob. The women sang the refrain a couple of times more but then they also resumed their seats.

For the following three hours not a soul stirred. No one prayed, sang, spoke or moved. A holy hush filled the entire church from front to back.

At 11:30pm no one had left the building. I looked across to one of the young women whose lifestyle I knew did not parallel with her Christian testimony. She was also sobbing.

As three hours had passed I quietly drew alongside her and asked if she was OK.

Without looking up to me, and with obvious reference to the young women from California in their unstylish clothes, she said through her tears, "It's the purity. I can't cope with the purity."

What commenced as the worst service we had ever attended had now become one of the best.

****

While this was taking place in the local church I continued as a member of Elim's Executive Council and travelled to Cheltenham for three days five times a year for the meetings.

Wynne Lewis, Elim's General Superintendent, was reaching the end of the second of his four-year terms and was about to retire from office and it was our responsibility as an Executive to nominate someone to succeed him.

The person nominated would then be put to the Conference for a vote that would be conducted by postal ballot and, to be confirmed in the role, the candidate would need the support of 66 per cent of the electorate.

The person chosen was someone who had occupied all the most senior roles within the Movement with the exception of General Superintendent. His name was John Smyth, an exceptional leader and the person who had afforded me so many opportunities in my ministry as well as being the one who had said those releasing words eighteen years earlier as I commenced as Regional Leader, "Go to Scotland and fulfil your ministry."

When the votes were counted John was just one vote short of the required majority and so was not elected.

The search for Wynne's successor recommenced.

Few if any would have considered me a candidate not least because of my age. John Smyth was sixty-four years old when he was approached as it was normal for someone in their early sixties to be considered. I was fifty-two.

I received in the post a letter from a colleague who, though not well known in the Movement or the minister of a large church, was one of the most affirming and encouraging people I had ever known and who, when he prophesied, was rarely wrong. Ray Jones had written to say that shortly I would be presented with a 'mountain that I would not have anticipated or ever expected to climb' adding that I should not shy away from accepting any challenge that presented itself.

10

Election as General Superintendent

Shortly after receiving the letter Wynne Lewis asked if I would be willing to let my name go forward to the Conference and subsequently I was elected as General Superintendent of the Elim Movement.

Not overly confident that I was equal to the task or qualified for such an honour, it was particularly encouraging to receive an unprecedented 93 per cent of the vote.

I would later go on to fulfil a total of four terms. The definition of the role is that of being the 'spiritual leader of the Movement with special responsibility for giving leadership to the National Leadership team'.

The guest speaker at the Conference in 2000 was Rev Dr Michael Ntumy who was the leader of the Church of Pentecost (CoP), in Ghana.

Trained many years earlier in our Elim College he was to take the CoP from a membership of around three quarters of a million to 1.3 million in his ten year tenure. Today CoP is over two million in membership and the largest of all denominations in Ghana. It is very ably led by the current Chairman Apostle Dr Opoku Onyinah who also trained in our college.

There is a very strong link between our two groups. For a time those CoP churches planted in the UK were called Elim Church of Pentecost and all their ministers in the UK received their ordination at our Conference. I have always had the highest regard for this great denomination.

In the service at the Conference at which the transfer of the role was to take place Dr Ntumy gave a powerful prophecy that impacted me greatly.

I later obtained a transcript of the prophecy but the part that was the most memorable was, "During your tenure there will be times when you will know no peace but do not be afraid for the Lord will give you the heart of a lion."

As I write this many years later there are two lion prints on our wall and two lion sculptures around the room. Our garden has a fountain with four lion faces and Marilyn even had my wedding ring remodelled with the head of a lion on it.

There are no other areas of my life that I have engaged in such symbolism. I felt, however, that this was a poignant prophecy and it proved to be so as time went by.

In the first week of taking up my role in Cheltenham I took John Smyth out for a meal. Apart from not reaching the required majority by just one vote he now had to come to Cheltenham and continue his role as Finance Director in the same building as the new GS. John could not have been more gracious in the entire time that we worked together before his retirement.

Simultaneously with commencing this new ministry Marilyn became very ill. She had had a big operation and, before she had adequately recovered from it, she had to have another. When she left hospital it was some weeks before she was strong enough to travel from Scotland and had to stay with an Elder and his wife. When she eventually joined me she was still very weak and the person who was the most support in those days was, of all people, Mary Smyth – John's wife. What a very special couple they were and still remain very close friends to this day.

****

I made a number of small immediate changes within the first few months of my tenure. The first was to take over as 'editor in chief' of our Movement's magazine *Direction*. Its change of style would herald in the minds of its readers the beginning of a change in culture.

Another apparently small thing was to change the name of the group of leaders who led the Movement between Conferences from the 'Executive Council' to the 'National Leadership Team' – which better reflected our new priorities as we moved from a sense of 'administering the denominational machine' to relationally leading the vision of a Movement.

Also, when the NLT met for three days five times a year we decided we would never treat stationing as 'just another item on the agenda'. Part of the responsibility of the NLT was marrying up churches looking for ministers with ministers looking for churches and we realised that the decisions we made would not just affect the minister and their spouse but also their family members who would be uprooted from schools and from close friends.

We committed from day one, and have never departed from it since, that when we reached this area on the agenda we would pause for a time of prayer asking for God's guidance and direction.

As important as these changes were there were many more radical changes that needed to be made if we were to successfully change culture. Too often organisations tinker around with cosmetic alterations, issue vision statements, implement programmes and change terminology under the illusion that they are making seismic shifts in direction. Usually all that materialises amounts to no more than rearranging the deckchairs on the Titanic or stone-cladding the walls of Jericho.

The largest shift of all was the need to change the focus from building bigger churches to, in the name of the book I wrote to underpin the new culture, *Building Bigger People*.

It is always a mistake to believe that the implementation of change is a reflection on the effectiveness of the culture that preceded one's own. My predecessor had been someone whose emphasis had been expressed in terms such as 'breaking barriers' and setting goals, targets and objectives. None of these, of course, are wrong in themselves but most heresy arises out of a truth that is taken to an unacceptable extreme. If numerical growth alone is the primary focus then people became little more than 'items of production' to fulfil the aspirations of leaders.

What is worse, those being led see themselves as of value only in proportion to the size of their churches or their ministries. When leaders met the opening sentences may include questions such as "How many did you have in on Sunday"? Or "How large is your budget?" People too easily can morph into statistics in such a climate.

There had been a time when it had been necessary to focus on numeric growth – so what had happened given that 'yesterday' was not wrong? The point was simply that 'yesterday' was right for yesterday but not for our current culture.

By changing the emphasis to 'building bigger people' we would still see growth but it would be growth that was sustainable. It was harder work but better work.

This involved actively looking for potential in others and giving them opportunity to grow deeper in God before endeavouring to accelerate their rise in status.

It was a culture of affirmation that valued character over charisma and integrity over talent while understanding that all these qualities were not mutually exclusive.

In the days when I had been a Regional Leader the principal of the college invited the NLT to meet with the students and in a panel format answer any questions that they had about their role. The purpose, I imagine, was to enable both groups to get to know one another better. Many of the students would have come from an Elim background and some would have been preparing to apply for the Elim ministry themselves.

As the session concluded the principal asked his students to articulate how they perceived the leadership styles of the five Regional leaders present. I cannot remember what was said about my colleagues other than that it was complimentary and that they were seen as spiritual men.

When it came to me the analysis was different. It was suggested that my style was that of a Premier League football manager who was looking for the best players, positioning them where they could do the most good and, between matches, training them to develop their skills further.

It was not a 'spiritual' analysis but one of the best compliments that I have ever received. As far as I was concerned they had 'got it in one'.

Some months before I had been elected, a residential centre had been booked for a theological conference. As important as theology is, no one on the NLT thought that theological debate was the primary priority of our new team at that juncture.

We were just about to cancel the venue when Bruce Hunter, who gave many years of sterling service to our Movement as Administrator, suggested that we retain the centre but hold instead a vision conference where I could unpack with our leaders our new vision and values and outline what our DNA as a Movement should be.

This was seen as an excellent idea and the conference took place with around four hundred of our key leaders in which we unpacked our vision of the future, listened to one another, shared in small groups and reconvened in plenary sessions.

I was overwhelmed with the degree of enthusiasm with which this new culture was being embraced and was extremely hopeful about the future.

It was at the first of these vision conferences that I introduced Elim's new logo.

Years earlier the Executive Council had talked about a logo but the idea had been eventually dismissed on the basis that, in order to be effective, every church would need to adopt it and it was considered unlikely that all would be willing to do so.

This assertion was based on the fact that, what was then termed as our Headquarters, were continually being asked by local churches if they could change their name as, so the argument went, 'no one knew what Elim meant'. As a result a plethora of new names emerged many of which had incorporated the words 'Community Church' or 'Christian Fellowship'.

I believed passionately in 'brand' and corporate identity but I knew that brand was not something that people could be coerced into. It was essential that the brand was linked to a culture that everyone wanted to identify with.

However I, and those working alongside me, were becoming increasingly aware that the Movement was now buying into the new vision and values that we were espousing.

Prior to the vision conference I had been speaking at the Elim Conference in New Zealand. After being picked up from the airport I was taken to the home of Luke and Marilyn Brough.

Luke was not only the leader of Elim New Zealand but also the senior pastor of the two thousand-strong Elim church in Auckland. Having been shown my room I returned to the lounge and noticed that the settee had a large board perched on it that was covered in paper.

When I asked Luke what this was he apologised, and moving it so I could take a seat said, "The Auckland church has just commissioned a top designer to create a logo for us and this is the result. It has just been delivered."

As he unveiled it I knew straight away that this was what I wanted to be adopted by Elim internationally.

Arriving home I asked Luke to send me the PDFs and pantone colours of the design. My colleagues on the NLT agreed with me that it was perfect and when I produced it for the first time at the vision conference it was enthusiastically received.

Our Conference not only universally adopted it but passed a resolution that it should be present not just on all signage in our churches but incorporated on all local and national publications.

What I found so encouraging at that time was not simply that we had secured a suitable logo but that the new Elim culture and corporate identity was being enthusiastically embraced.

It is now virtually unheard of for any church to change their name to something that does not have Elim in the title. On the contrary, when new local name changes are registered, almost without exception it is because they wish the name 'Elim' to be incorporated back into the title.

I am forever grateful for Elim New Zealand's generosity in allowing what was originally intended for a local church to be rolled out to thousands of other Elim churches around the world.

* * * * * * * * * * * * * * * *

I realised that if the principle of 'building bigger people' was right for others it also had to be part of who I was. I had been given a huge electoral mandate from our conference and had at that time the unequivocal support of the NLT. It was essential therefore that I build boundaries around my own life and became mutually accountable to others who could speak into my life and with whom I could confide.

There had been a small group in London that met and consisted of two people who I already knew well. They had met for some time for fellowship and a good meal but most of all to pray for one another and to be mutually transparent.

At one time a great friend of our Movement, RT Kendall, then minister of Westminster Chapel, had been a part of the group but he had now moved back to the States. Another had taken his place who also had left and I was approached and asked if I would make up the group of four.

I readily agreed.

The facilitator of the small band was Lyndon Bowring who, while being the Chairman of CARE was also an ordained Elim minister and someone who had already been a friend for thirty years and with whom I would often share a room at our annual conference if our wives were not with us. I believe Lyndon to be one of the most influential evangelicals in the UK.

The second person was Jeff Lucas. He had begun his ministry as an Elim minister and at one point we had considered working alongside one another in the days when I was the pastor in Cheltenham. He later became part of the Pioneer Network of churches led by Gerald Coates and was then sharing his time three ways – occupying the teaching role at a nine thousand strong AoG church in Colorado during the time he was in the USA, leading Spring Harvest and touring as a conference speaker.

Jeff is one of the most prolific Christian authors on both sides of the Atlantic and, in my view, one of the best communicators I had ever heard. Most of all he was, and is, a great friend.

The third person in the group was entirely unknown to me except by reputation but someone who I grew to respect, value and hugely appreciate in the years that we got to know one another. At that time David Coffey was the General Secretary of the Baptist Union and later became the President of the World Baptist Alliance during which five year tenure he was awarded an OBE.

I cannot adequately express how important these three became over the years that ensued. Our openness to one another and the vulnerability that allowed us to be real created a safe place in which one could be both challenged and affirmed. Amongst ourselves we referred to this group as the Gang of Four and, more often than not, met at Lyndon's office in Westminster.

When I was meeting other people on business in the London area I would sometimes meet them at the Carlton Club in St James' Street around the corner from the Ritz. I was a member of the International Club that used the Carlton Club's facilities. The Carlton Club is set in a beautiful Georgian house and was formed in 1832 as a men-only club.

The first time I attended I noticed that the person who had signed in prior to myself was Baroness Thatcher for whom the club had made an exception when she was Prime Minister.

Election as General Superintendent

A couple of years later, having been in the lounge with someone who had joined me as a guest, I moved on to the dining room for a meal. On our return I went to regain my favourite spot to discover it was occupied by David Cameron and his guest.

The significance of this was that he had refused to join the Carlton Club as it was a men only establishment. The previous day it had changed the rule to allow women members who now had access to most of the rooms. He was clearly there to make a point as his guest was a woman.

It was around the time that I came into office that women were allowed to be ordained in Elim.

When the Movement was formed in 1915 women were very much part of this new expression of church. However, when Elim initiated ordination it was only men, for some reason, that were invited to apply.

I had been brought up as a child in a world in which it was taken for granted that spiritual leadership was male. My father was Irish and traditional in his views. My mother never attended church without wearing a hat. It was even some years before a TV was allowed in the house and, even then, no one was allowed to watch it on a Sunday.

A bizarre moment occurred on the occasion that my parents took us as small children on holiday to a northern seaside resort.

As it was Sunday my father sought out a Pentecostal church. As there was not an Elim church in the town we attended one of another denomination. I was about eleven at the time which made my two sisters eight and six respectively.

It was an intolerably hot day and we arrived at the church during the singing of the opening hymn. I entered the row first followed by my sisters, our mother and my father took his place at the seat by the aisle. The hymn having concluded the minister announced that the meeting could not continue as people were present who were inappropriately attired.

I looked around in the hope that someone had come in wearing a swimming costume but was disappointed to see this was not the case. It then occurred to me that perhaps a woman was not wearing a hat. I did a quick assessment of the congregation but saw that everyone, including my mother, was wearing one. It was then that I saw a cadaverous deacon approaching with two plastic rain hoods in his hand which he offered to my father to pass on to my two little sisters.

The stand-off between the deacon and my father must have lasted only a matter of seconds but it seemed like an eternity. My father, with every eye in the small congregation on him, refused to accept the proffered offering and eventually the deacon shuffled away and the meeting resumed.

Even at that young age I wondered what would have happened if someone had not been as resolute as my father and little girls had been forced to sit there with these appendages on their heads when it was 90 degrees in the shade.

Or far worse, what if we had been a family of non-Christians coming to church for the first time?

The matter of women's ministry was never an issue in our house. My mother would preach not only in my father's church but at women's conventions across the country.

Women in church leadership was, however, an issue.

My personal questioning of the authenticity of such a position came by asking myself the question, "How could it be that the same denominations that forbade women from leading churches in this country would totally support and finance them to go to the most dangerous parts of the world as missionaries to lead and teach others?" Such a position had to be totally untenable.

I, of course, respect those who hold a different point of view but from that moment I supported the concept that not only should women be in ministry but also in leadership.

Elim's culture dramatically changed in those early years but our structure still needed to become more flexible.

The contrast I concluded was similar to that between a railway and a river.

I imagined one of those early steam trains that traversed huge spaces across the American prairies. As my mind embraced the scene I saw a huge boulder that had become lodged on the track. The driver, with a clear line of sight, is able to see the obstacle and slow down. Having stopped the train he is then able to call in engineers to remove the boulder and, this having been done, the train is able to slowly resume its speed.

Now I imagined that same heavy obstruction in the middle of a small river. The torrent of water is hardly impeded at all as it simply meanders towards the obstacle and navigates its way around it.

What if a whole Movement could operate like that? What if every obstacle was viewed as an opportunity?

The biggest 'what if' of all was shortly to materialise.

The Best is Yet to Come

11

What If?

$\mathbf{A}$ couple of years into my first term as General Superintendent I boarded a train at Paddington and was looking forward to occupying myself by commencing a book someone had given to me earlier in the day.

Instead of opening at the first page I found myself looking at a blank page inside the front cover.

I immediately felt the Holy Spirit speak to me and say, "What if Elim was not a ninety year old denomination but was commencing today with a blank page? What would God want to write in that new space?"

I retrieved a pen and began writing in response to what I believed the Lord was saying. What I placed on the page is not the reason why this is recorded here. What was more important was the initial sense I had of how we, and all Christian organisations for that matter, should approach understanding the will of God.

Too often what was categorised as 'guidance' could really be reduced to an attempt to get God on our agenda and, having done so, pray that he provides the resources for its implementation.

It now occurred to me that what was more important was for us to recognise God's agenda and align with it in the knowledge that he always resources his purposes.

As far as our Movement was concerned four questions needed to be asked:

- What did God want to accomplish in the nation?

- What is the shape of the tool that will accomplish what God wants to do in the nation?

- How far is Elim from the shape of that tool?

- What is Elim willing to die to in order to become the shape of the tool that will accomplish what God wants to do in the nation?

It so happened that a few days later an NLT meeting was scheduled to take place.

Each of the three days begin with up to an hour that includes someone bringing a word followed by a time of prayer. All eleven of us take it in turns to lead these devotions and I was scheduled to take the first of these.

Our business sessions are usually conducted around a boardroom table, but the times of seeking God together take place in a separate lounge area. It was in that context that I shared what had happened on the train. I commenced by outlining the above four stages followed by a deeper analysis of what I believed were the radical structural changes needed to create the necessary new wineskins.

I was eager to preface my conclusions by saying that it was premature to bring these things 'to the table' because of their potentially disruptive nature.

It was unanimously felt, however, that this was something that God had initiated and should be discussed without delay. I pointed out that, were these concepts to be embraced, it may mean that the roles of those in the room may drastically change and some may even have to move on to other areas of ministry.

The quality of the people I was working with was again evidenced by the unanimous sense that God's purpose superseded all personal considerations.

What If?

At the next vision conference these changes were discussed in small groups and plenary sessions and it was clear that the vast majority of our leaders were on board. However, the constitutional changes took four years to pass through conference before everything was put in place.

I not only felt that we were starting with a 'blank piece of paper' but also realised that the changes would release two hundred thousand pounds of 'old money' every year towards our new priorities – amounts that were in place before any fresh revenue needed to be raised.

The ripples that reverberated from these core decisions affected many areas of our Movement's life but two only need be mentioned here.

We had a fine theological college with a first class principal and faculty. However, we began to realise that while over the years we had been educating people to 'know' it was equally essential that we trained people to 'do'. And this training should not be confined to pastoral leaders of churches but the training of leaders at every strata of our Movement's life.

We invited one of our finest leaders, Nigel Tween, to be Elim's first 'Director of Training', a role that he would fulfil for ten years. Every aspect of training, the college included, would come under his remit and during his term he would oversee the training options within Elim by making training operate remotely and the conduits of interaction with training more diverse.

During his term he would set up chaplaincy training for those in hospitals, prisons, schools, the fire service and the armed forces. When Nigel moved on to his next phase of ministry Dave Newton, who had been in senior leadership in *British Youth for Christ*, took over the role and very quickly made it his own by taking Movement-wide training to yet another level.

The second area that we prioritised was youth. We had previously had a youth department which at that time was run by a fine leader, Roger Rowland. However, it was massively underfunded and when

Roger took on another area of ministry what became known as *Serious4God* (*S4G*) came into being.

The person who spearheaded this was Mark Pugh. Mark had begun as a worship leader and at this point was an associate pastor. Mark and his wife, Nita, were people of the highest calibre and perfect for a role that would become one of the most exciting aspects of Elim in years to come.

From the start the impetus of this new youth initiate was amazing but something was about to happen that would accelerate the department exponentially.

One day Mark asked to meet me saying he had a proposition to make. The question he put was, "John, what if we could see a thousand young people make a first-time commitment to Christ in just a single day?"

My first thought was to ask myself at what event in my lifetime had I ever seen that take place in the UK. I could not think of any.

My first question, however, revolved around the fact that in his last event 1,700 people had been present drawn from Elim churches in the area and the vast majority of them would already be Christians. To see a thousand new commitments would need many more people in attendance.

Mark had already thought that through and then presented me with the next "What if?"

"What if the NLT were willing to invest £20,000 over a weekend with the knowledge that they would not get the money back?" Apparently he had in mind that the event would cost around £70,000 of which £50,000 would materialise from ticket sales. The idea was to take a five thousand seater space in the National Exhibition Centre in Birmingham.

On the basis of Mark's track record the NLT agreed and months of preparation began by the *S4G* team.

Just a few days before the event I was in an NLT meeting when my phone vibrated – the screen revealing an urgent text from Mark, "Seating number problem, please phone."

What If?

Knowing we were already £20,000 down, and that if this place was not packed the deficit could be far greater, I hit the reply button with not a little disquiet.

There was indeed a seating problem and I learned that, five thousand tickets already having been sold, Mark was having to ask the NEC to reconfigure the number of seats available.

It was an amazing event. A well-known band provided the music and Mark Ritchie brought a tremendous evangelistic message.

When Mark made the appeal, however, no one moved. A few moments later someone stood to their feet who, looking around to see that they were on their own in the vast auditorium, promptly sat down again.

Nevertheless, within a short time people began not just to stand but to move towards the front. It was without doubt one of the most poignant moments in my entire life as I witnessed the number of people who signified that they were making a first time decision for Christ.

When Mark and I first met to discuss this event he had said he believed that a thousand young people could come to Christ in a day. The number who signed decision cards that day were one thousand one hundred and thirty seven.

After ten years leading *S4G* Mark went on to lead the Rediscover Church in Exeter and Tim Alford took up his role and continues to do an amazing job in that capacity.

It was during this same period that another innovation took place.

Marilyn has been relentlessly supportive of my ministry throughout our marriage. I never once remember her complaining of the time that I had to spend on the road, though she did sometimes question the effect it may be having on me.

She travelled with me continually when I preached at the weekends though we agreed from the outset that a proportion of weekends needed to be based in the local church in Cheltenham where she could maintain friendships and sit under the excellent ministry of the pastor, Gareth Lewis, the son of my predecessor.

On those occasions that she did not accompany me I was often aware as I entered the venue where I was preaching that the pastor, and especially his wife, would be looking over my shoulder with the words, "Oh, Marilyn is not with you!" I often told her I believed people looked forward far more to seeing her than they did me.

Marilyn is the kind of person that other women feel free to open up to. I have lost count of the occasions when we have been in public places and noticed her missing only to then discover that a perfect stranger is chatting to her and seemingly telling her their life story. She welcomes such moments rather than recoiling from them.

In 2012 Marilyn was diagnosed with breast cancer. When, in his tiny office, the consultant gave us the news neither he nor we at that time knew how far the disease had spread. He expressed sympathetically but firmly that if the disease of this grade had spread to other organs or glands the prognosis would be serious.

We were now faced with a 'What if?' of an entirely different kind.

I wondered at the time why, given that the consulting room was so small, a nurse needed to be present. I later discovered, given that people responded to the news they were being given in so many different ways, she needed to be there as a support either for the patient or the consultant. Sometimes a patient would faint and other times respond hysterically – even aggressively regaling the doctor with the unfairness of it all.

Marilyn's even temperament as she received the news brought the doctor to the conclusion she had not taken in what he had said.

Reassuring him that she had Marilyn added, "Whatever happens it will be a win-win situation. As I am a Christian I believe I can be healed. If, however, through your skills I come through the operation well I will be fine. If on the other hand my situation is terminal I do not believe that death is the end and so I shall go home to be with the Lord."

I had heard Marilyn speak at conferences about the God who is as faithful in the valleys as the mountain tops. Now I was witnessing her living out that faith not in a pulpit but in the place where it really mattered – the crucible of harsh reality.

Everything did turn out well. The cancer had not spread to the lymph glands and the operation was a success. When, weeks later and in the same room, we thanked the consultant for all he had done he replied, "Only fifty per cent of your recovery had to do with my skills. The other fifty per cent had to do with the raw material I had to work with."

Neither of us would contend that every 'what if?' in our marriage and ministry has been handled with overcoming faith. Sometimes doubts and disappointments have appeared almost overwhelming but, even at those times, God is faithful.

In 2007 Marilyn founded Elim's first national women's ministry called *Aspire*. Working with a great team who are numbered among her closest friends, it has born much fruit and affected the lives of women of all ages.

In 2015 Mark Lyndon Jones commenced Elim's first men's ministry *Mpower*. This gifted leader and fine pastor has brought much added-value to our Movement through this ministry.

The Best is Yet to Come

12

Strengths and Weaknesses

I was now in my second term as the leader of the Movement. My first term had been for four years and I was gratified by the level of trust that delegates had put in me by granting me such a clear mandate.

I realised, however, that after four years in the role any 'honeymoon' was long over and knew that some of the decisions I had made would not have been universally popular. To my great surprise therefore my second term began with a vote increased from 93 per cent to 96 per cent.

When I was put forward for an unprecedented third term my vote fell by 9 per cent to 87 per cent and, while this was a clear mandate, it was a reflection of some tensions that were arising that also made their presence felt on the NLT.

Throughout most of Elim's life the way that anyone got on the NLT was by a nomination from the floor of Conference. Anyone was eligible and, when vacancies occurred, those who allowed their name to go forward and achieved the highest vote were elected. There were strengths and weaknesses with this.

The strength was that it was an egalitarian process. The weakness was that those with the highest profile in the Movement were selected and those who were eminently suitable, but unknown by most, were overlooked.

The Conference debated the process and decided that the GS should nominate those he wanted on his team but that those nominated must also receive a clear mandate from the Conference.

In the first year that the responsibility to nominate fell to me I made a conscious decision not to populate the team with those who were entirely behind the new culture that had been implemented during my term.

I considered it healthy that those who had opposing views were able to articulate their concerns as perhaps those same positions would be present in the wider Movement and everyone, I felt, should feel that their views were likely to be represented within the National Leadership Team.

Eric McComb, the then Irish Superintendent, who I considered a friend and was a good man, had views that most certainly did not parallel with my own. I felt it right nevertheless to include him on my team.

Though this may have been healthy it did mean that some of the principles that I held to be important had to be fought for if the values that I was seeking to inculcate could be solidified.

Tensions came to the fore around the time the NLT had to make a decision whether or not they would present my name to Conference for a third term.

In my view, those who opposed me knew that the Conference would be almost certain to re-elect me and so had a dilemma. When the secret ballot among the NLT was counted, though no one had voted against me, three people chose to abstain – the same number that had abstained when I was first put forward to the Movement as General Superintendent eight years earlier.

Not all the tension in those months came from the opposition of those who were against the direction I was taking Elim. Some of it was of my own making.

I have always been a person to run to a challenge rather than away from it. If I have toothache my inclination is to go straight to the dentist preferring short-term pain to longer term inconvenience. If there is tension in a room I would be more likely to recognise it and address it rather than hoping it might go away.

I certainly do not relish confrontation for its own sake but I am well aware that if my car cannot move to my destination without the friction between the tyre and the road, some rough terrain has to be engaged with in leadership if progress is to be made and worthwhile destinations are to be reached.

I have always believed that a good gardener must not only love flowers but also be willing to grasp nettles.

I also contend that leaders whose primary goal in ministry is to lead a quiet life are occupying a position that would be better filled by someone else.

I have no doubt that during those difficult seasons there would have been times when, rather than softening the discussion, I 'raised the ante' by pushing my proposals harder and further.

These days I am perhaps a little more circumspect and, though I hope my tread is every bit as sure-footed, it tends to land a little lighter.

As I read scripture I find that people's strengths are also their potential weaknesses. Samson's strength was his physical prowess but his testosterone-fuelled encounters were also the source of his difficulties.

From an opposite vantage point I remember attending the farewell service of a Church of Scotland minister who had come to the church as a student from seminary and was leaving fifty years later in retirement.

During the service the principal Elder paid tribute to the minister's personal deportment by saying that there had never been a disagreement in the church session in the entire period and that their minister was the 'most gracious man in Scotland'.

On the following Monday morning I was sitting in a cafe with a young minister who had asked to see me when I noticed the recently retired minister coming in through the door.

Realising that he was alone, and wanting to affirm him in front of my young friend, I introduced him with the words, "Come and meet the most gracious man in Scotland."

I expected a smile or a dismissive wave that would swat away my compliment with his characteristic humility. As he joined us, however, his face was grave and he said as he sat, "It's true we never had a confrontational moment in our leadership meetings – but there was many a time when we should have done. I was inducted into a small congregation and fifty years later I have left a small congregation. If I had not been so afraid of confrontation I would have left a far larger number to be pastored by my successor."

In my sixteen-year tenure I experienced very little resistance to change within the Movement with the notable exception of that which came from the Irish churches – especially those in the north of Ireland.

I understand the Irish culture and mentality given that I am half Irish myself.

Elim in Ireland from the earliest days had a separate constitution that laid out a small number of areas in which it was permitted to have autonomy. However, in every respect, apart from those few prescribed areas, the churches were under the authority of the wider Movement. When Elim ministers, after a five year training period, are ordained they make a public commitment to unreservedly abide by the decisions made by the wider Conference and that includes leaders from Ireland.

During my tenure, however, especially during the latter half, fault lines between Ireland and the rest of the Movement began to reveal themselves. The tensions had always been there but up until the half-way mark the then Irish Superintendent had a place on the National Leadership Team and therefore exerted an influence over the wider Movement. When he retired that influence was no longer there.

This is not to say that Ireland is not represented on the NLT as it currently has two Irishmen among its number. One born in the North and the other in the South.

What had been taking place, however, over time was that the Irish Superintendent appeared to be encouraging the development of a Movement within a Movement.

Historically Irish churches did not support the wider Movement financially in the way that other churches did. Churches in England, Scotland and Wales tithed their offerings to the Movement while the Irish churches gave only a small nominal amount. They justified this on the basis that they did not look to the wider Elim Movement to provide the salary of its Superintendent or the provision of a suite of offices for him.

Before my tenure had commenced the Irish churches were granted permission to publish their own magazine with the understanding it would run alongside Elim's Movement-wide magazine *Direction*. However, within a short time the purchase of *Direction* had decreased to the point that no more than two hundred copies were sold in the whole country and, in parallel with this, virtually no report of any events outside of Ireland, were mentioned in the Irish publication.

There was a period when there was not even a link on the Irish website that acknowledged that Elim existed outside its own borders – though it has to be said that when this was pointed out a link was inserted.

The next contributing factor was that Elim, nationally, had become a member of *Churches Together in England* (CTE). Ireland's problem with that was that among the thirty two denominations represented one of them was the Roman Catholic Church.

The Irish churches attempted to reverse this in a subsequent national Conference. The meeting was, without doubt, one of the most difficult that I had been called upon to chair as there were several occasions when rules of debate were ignored as the Irish delegates vociferously aired their strongly held views.

However, so overwhelming was the feeling of Conference against the Irish proposal to withdraw from CTE that a motion was passed to simply 'move to the next business' and only a handful of delegates out of the several hundred present voted against that motion.

I have always believed that the building of bridges is better than the erecting of barricades and it has always amazed me that it has been the belief of some that when a Catholic and a Pentecostal are in conversation that the outcome is most likely to be that the Pentecostal will be set 'on the road to Rome' rather than the Catholic being brought into a fuller understanding of the Pentecostal's perspective.

Ecumenism has nothing to do with coming 'under the influence of others' but of listening to others with courtesy and respect in an atmosphere devoid of ill feeling.

It is perhaps significant that at the close of the first CTE meeting of denominational leaders I attended in London that I was approached by the Chair who, after expressing appreciation of the membership of Elim, said, "You know, John, many of the leaders here today will be unaware of the work of the Holy Spirit across the world though the Pentecostal Churches. Would you be willing to address that subject at length at our next meeting?"

I was unable to attend on the specified date but Nigel Tween took up the responsibility and was warmly and enthusiastically received.

The biggest problem, however, that the Irish churches had was the ordination of women. Although this had been passed sixteen years earlier Ireland refused to comply with it. There were several Irish pastors in favour of the recognition of the leadership of women but, as many of them were of a younger generation and secret ballots were rarely taken, some appeared intimidated into an assent to the status quo.

In order to address the matters referred to above and seek to reconcile the issues, the NLT offered to travel to Ireland to see if progress could be made and in consequence all eleven members of the NLT travelled to Hillsborough for what turned out to be a three-hour meeting. It proved unproductive.

Some have asked why I chose to address the issue just prior to my election to what would prove to be an unprecedented fourth term of office. Would it not have been better, it was implied, to secure the vote first?

This was never a consideration as I have always attempted to do what I considered to be right rather than succumb to short-term political expediency.

When the vote was taken the Movement gave me an 84 per cent mandate. Had no Irish vote been included in the count it would most certainly have been considerably higher.

****

The bridges between Elim and our sister fellowship, the Assemblies of God, have always been strong and their General Superintendents I have numbered among my closest friends notably Warwick Shenton, Paul Weaver and John Partington.

All three of them were very different in their leadership style and each brought their particular gifts to the growth and development of their denomination.

There was always a sense that they wanted the best for Elim as we in Elim certainly wanted God's best for them – and of course still do. There is an absence of competitiveness between both groups. The difference between us is structural rather than doctrinal. Elim is centrally governed and the Assemblies of God are a fellowship of autonomous churches. All Elim assets, including property, is owned centrally and in AoG it is not.

I have very few regrets in my life and most of those that I have would be private. But if I have one that can be shared it is that our two Movements did not come even closer together.

I believe that wish was also in the hearts of each of the AoG leaders I have mentioned. But the 'longest engagement in history' as some called it never became a marriage.

Relationship-building outside of Pentecostal and Charismatic circles was never a priority in the earlier part of my ministry. As a young leader I was preoccupied with what was happening within our own network. However, a catalytic moment, that does not at all reflect well on me, took place at a *Spring Harvest* meeting and was to radically transform my perspective.

I have spoken at the *Spring Harvest* main stage in what is known as the Big Top, but that is not the event that retained any particular resonance for me.

Two years before that I had been invited to speak at one of the smaller venues to a group of just a few hundred people. It was my first *Spring Harvest* engagement.

As I sat on the front row next to a young lady who was to convene the service, and later introduce me, I cast an eye over the congregation.

They were clearly not the people I was used to preaching to and, as the opening songs were being sung, it was evident by the style of worship that there were very few of my 'tribe' present.

I became aware of the development of a critical attitude in my spirit and wondered why I had been chosen to speak to a group with whom I felt I had so little in common.

When the convenor asked me what form of appeal I would be likely to make at the conclusion of my message I wanted to say, "I can't imagine eliciting a response from anyone in this room," but of course that was not articulated. I simply avoided the question by saying, "I am happy to leave that with you."

It was around fifteen minutes prior to when I was due to be introduced that I experienced what was one of the strongest senses of rebuke from the Holy Spirit that I can remember feeling at any point in my life to that point.

It was as if God had opened up my heart to see it in all its pretence and arrogance. The moment was so strong that I almost felt physically ill. I just about composed myself as I came to the microphone but not before I had repented of my judgemental attitude.

Strengths and Weaknesses

Even as I write this many years later I find it hard to put into words the significance of that encounter with God. No vocabulary could adequately express it.

When I concluded, the convenor invited anyone to whom God had spoken during my message to come to the front and write their thoughts on one of numerous pads of yellow *post-it* notes that had been provided. They were then asked to stick these responses to a large wooden cross at the front of the auditorium apparently placed there for this purpose.

Scores of people made their way forward and very soon the wooden structure was obliterated in a riot of yellow.

I had been asked to speak on the subject "Jesus, Light of the World" but, without a shadow of a doubt, the person who had been the subject of heaven's laser gaze the most was myself – and certainly the one who received the most illumination.

This pivotal point was the place when I developed a far greater respect and regard for those who worshipped in a different tradition from my own who, from that day on, I would find myself not just 'talking at' but actively 'listening to'.

Pentecostal and Charismatics are great 'transmitters'. We pride ourselves in our ability to proclaim what we believe in testimony and have little reticence in uninhibitedly expressing ourselves to God in worship. We are not always as good, in my opinion, as acting as 'receivers'. This is something we could with profit learn from those of other traditions who understand the value of quietness and refection more than we sometimes do.

There is, perhaps, a sense of irony in the fact that a few years later, during the days that Joel Edwards was its Director, I was asked to become a member of Council of the *Evangelical Alliance* – a group that represents two million Evangelicals and eighty-one denominations.

Ten years later I was elected Chair of Council – the first Pentecostal to hold that position in its 169 year history and to become a member of its Board. It was a particular honour to act as Chair during the major realignment of the Council in 2016.

I have nothing but admiration for the work of the Alliance. Its Director, Steve Clifford, is one of the finest spiritual statesmen and gracious individuals that I have ever met. He is also a much valued friend.

13

Pivotal People

I am sometimes asked by those outside of Elim why, given that I support women in leadership, there are no women on the National Leadership Team.

One of the reasons for this is that, though the ordination of women was brought in in 1999, the Conference did not permit women to be part of the National leadership Team until 2014.

Working alongside the NLT during my term of office has without doubt been one of the greatest joys of my role. Their loyalty and support, especially during the past eight years, has been an unqualified pleasure.

I have often said that Elim has an 'embarrassment of riches' when it comes to leadership, and every four years when it fell to me to nominate those who would serve alongside me, I found it an almost impossible task.

As this book will be read by many outside our own family of churches, and several on the NLT have ministries far wider than our denomination, I will introduce some that I have not mentioned previously.

David Campbell is the leader of the two Metropolitan regions and covers the largest number of churches. Some years ago he commenced an annual event called *Rivercamp* that meets near Evesham and attracts around two thousand people. I have massively valued his insight, wisdom and loyalty over the many years he has been in senior leadership.

Kevin Peat, who covers Scotland and the North West of England, carries such a pastoral heart for leaders that I considered him almost irreplaceable when I was in office.

Simon Foster, who is Regional Leader for Wales and the South West, has pastored some of our largest churches and is, without doubt, one of the most prophetic people I know. The value of his input has been incalculable.

Many would consider Duncan Clark and James Glass to be perfect examples of what is being referred to these days as the 'Quiet Leader'. Though they both lead large and significant churches they do not feel the need to address every subject that arises on the agenda but, when they choose to speak, I notice the body language of those around them as they 'lean forward' to better hear the contribution that they make.

When I first came into office I set up a group called the 'GS Forum' which was comprised of leaders of churches with more than four hundred in attendance. There was a three-fold purpose in this. The first was that I could listen to them, the second that I could share with them in advance of the wider Movement some of the plans that I intended to implement. The third was so that these busy people could meet, and get to know, people with a similar level of responsibility.

When all thirty-five of them were in the room they represented over twenty thousand of our Movement's constituency around the UK.

This group was later developed into what was called *'The Bridge'*. The difference was that the first group was augmented to include those who did not have large churches currently but who, in my opinion, would be leading large congregations within the next few years.

The Bridge also included women leaders and leaders from significant ethnic churches in our Movement. Although we only met for two days twice a year I found it a dynamic forum to be part of. Without doubt some of the thinking that arose from within our time together found its way onto the agenda of the NLT and was later adopted by the Movement as a whole.

Elim has a presence in forty countries around the world and, while I considered my primary responsibility was being with our churches in the UK, there were occasions when I would travel to special events organised by our International Missions Directors – formerly Chris Jones and currently Paul Hudson.

Not wanting to engage in a long list of very many trips, highlights would include Brazil, France, Ghana, Italy and New Zealand.

Each Missions Director has brought their own flavour and gift to their role but I consider Paul Hudson to be outstanding in his pastoral care for our international family of churches around the world.

Virtually all my weekends were engaged with our churches in the UK. I cannot remember any period when my appointments were not booked sixteen months in advance and at one point this extended to two years.

Although preaching in our churches, large and small, helped me to appreciate what was being achieved by our leaders and congregations around the UK and Ireland, the most significant part of the day for me was after the Sunday morning service had concluded and I could mix with the people before having lunch with the pastors and their spouses before travelling back home.

I have mentioned a number of pivotal people who are household names within Elim and now I will mention some people who are very special to Marilyn and I although they may be unlikely to have featured on many conference platforms.

Almost as soon as I had been elected in October 1999 I was approached by a woman pastor who was then on the team of Kensington Temple in London. June Freudenberg said that she was offering to set up a 'prayer shield' for Marilyn and I as we travelled and "was this something that I would welcome?"

She together with Diane Druce, the pastor of our church in Barnet, set up a team of people, mostly from her church, who committed to pray for us at every ministry appointment that I would be engaged. As each year began I gave them my appointments twelve months in advance in the certain knowledge that prayer covering would be received.

They did this throughout my entire tenure of sixteen years and, when I retired from my role in 2016, they made a further commitment to cover me in prayer as I itinerated during the years that followed. I am immeasurably indebted to them.

Alistair Cole, who has done such an amazing job of heightening the role of intercession in Elim, has also regularly encouraged the Movement to pray for us.

Much of my working week was based in Cheltenham and latterly Malvern – the move to which I will mention later.

It would be impossible to mention all those I had the privilege of working alongside over the years.

I have already mentioned our Administrator, Bruce Hunter, but it would be impossible not to highlight the sterling service given by Robert Millar our Finance Director whose wisdom I relied on on many occasions.

His wife, Sharon, was my PA and words fail me to express how much I have depended on her administrative skills and consummate professionalism. More important than even this, however, is the gracious way that she represented my department to the wider Movement. No ordination service ever took place where candidates failed to mention the help that Sharon had been to them during their years as 'ministers in training'.

One area of frustration for me was that, even with speaking at churches every weekend and at Regional meetings in the week, it was still very difficult to interface with almost a thousand pastors throughout the UK and Ireland.

At the beginning of one year I made what turned out to be an extremely rash promise. I said that within the next twelve months I would phone every pastor once and every 'minister in training' twice simply to ask how they were doing.

I considered this feasible as it seemed a simple enough task to pick up the phone between appointments or when waiting at airports for a flight.

That was until I realised that I had committed to making more than two thousands extra phone calls within a year. I fulfilled that promise over the next twelve month period but never embarked on the enterprise again.

One day my PA informed me that a small group of our principal worship leaders in Elim had booked an appointment to see me. All I was told was that Sam Blake, Stephen Gibson, Joel Pridmore and Ian Yates would be coming though nothing was said as to why the meeting had been set up.

When the day arrived, and just moments before they came into my office, the Lord spoke to me clearly. As they were ushered into the room and shown to their seats I opened the conversation by saying, "Good to see you guys, the Lord has just said I should say that whatever your question is the answer is 'yes'."

Understandably I had never in my life said that to anyone previously and certainly have never done so since.

They said that when Elim commenced almost a century earlier our beginnings were marked by three things, two of which were known to most people. George Jeffreys had held huge evangelistic services around the country in which thousands of people had come to Christ. Secondly, these meetings had been accompanied by hundreds of documented instances of Divine healing.

The reason why these four young men had come was to remind me that there was a third factor – the emergence of a new genre of music that, apart from being an inspirational aspect of those revival meetings, also communicated the vision and values of this rapidly emerging Movement.

This begged the question, "Was there not now a need to express through our music the essence of what God was accomplishing at this point in our history? What were the cardinal truths we wanted to convey today?"

It was at this moment that *Elim Sound* was conceived. Since then they have produced several albums and award-winning songs that are now well known across the wider church. They have also produced a worship resource for children, have set up training opportunities around the country and online and now have a fully financially resourced department.

At all our major conferences and events *Elim Sound*, augmented by many other top musicians, provide the music. I am immensely proud of every one of them and the birth of *Elim Sound* remains one of the highlights of my period in office.

14

Four Pivotal Events

Before my tenure as General Superintendent had begun in 2000, and while I was a member of the NLT, consideration was given to bringing our Administrative Headquarters, Theological College and Conference Centre together in one geographical location. The timing, however, never seemed right and, most importantly, the right venue did not become available.

A week before Christmas 2010 I received a phone call from Nigel Tween to say that a friend of his, who was an agent for properties at the high end of the market, had told him that St James' College, West Malvern, had come on the market. The site stretched over a massive thirty four acres that included several large buildings, a theatre and even a row of Edwardian houses.

If this was suitable it could prove to be the ideal location for what we had in mind so I and a few colleagues set up an immediate appointment to view.

We were told that the girls' college had been known for charging the highest school fees in the country – higher even than the prestigious Cheltenham Ladies' College or Roedean.

I well remember on our initial visit walking into the chemistry lab which seemed almost identical to the facility I remembered fifty years earlier in my old Grammar School – dark oak table tops replete with Bunsen burners and all the accoutrements of a science lab from the early 1960s. I asked how long the school had been empty and was told to my surprise that it was operating up until just six weeks previously.

This gave us some indication of the amount of investment we would need to put in place beyond the purchase price of the properties and the grounds.

Early in the New Year I called a special meeting of the NLT and we met at what was then our Theological College in Nantwich.

We needed to hear clearly from God on the matter as the financial investment would be huge.

Apart from the purchase of the site we now knew that it would take a year to internally demolish much of what was in place and a further year to build it to the standard that we required. The renovation cost alone would prove to be in excess of five million pounds.

By the end of the day, and after a great deal of thought and prayer, we decided to proceed with the purchase.

One of the things that was in the forefront of our minds was that, while we knew that if we went ahead this would be the largest Pentecostal Centre in Europe, we most certainly did not want to fall into the trap of creating a status symbol – an ecclesiastical obelisk that pandered to our egos.

We knew that if the enterprise was to be entered into it must only be because it was the will of God and created a tool for future generations that would better serve the purpose of extending the Kingdom of God.

We felt clear that God was in this and so we proceeded to the point of purchase.

When our acquisition had become public knowledge, but before any work on the properties had commenced, Nigel Tween who was at that time the Director of Training and a prominent NLT member asked to see me.

He suggested that the purchase may appear threatening to some of the residents who lived in the vicinity given that we appeared to be buying up most of West Malvern. It was possible that they may be anxious about the effect it could have upon them. Issues in their mind may include traffic management and the incursion into the area of a great many staff and students.

Also, it was likely that most of them would have little knowledge about Elim beyond what they had Googled. Some might even be worried that we were a cult.

One of the properties we had purchased was a theatre and this seemed to be the best venue to hold a public meeting.

Members of the local council and a representative from the police were invited together with any interested parties.

We asked the councillors how many residents usually turned up to any public meeting that they called. They told us, "About half a dozen."

The entire theatre was packed with not a seat to spare.

I introduced our departmental heads and asked them to briefly explain what they did. Those present were not aware, for example, that of the 190,000 charities in the UK Elim was in the top fifty in terms of revenue. Nor did they know that our work overseas included running medical clinics, schools and providing disaster relief.

We went to great lengths to say that, not only would the site not be detrimentally affected, but that the grounds and environment would be enhanced.

I should point out that our International Centre is situated at the top of the nine-mile stretch of the Malvern Hills.

From my office window I could see on a clear day fifty miles to the mountains of Wales. Within the property that we had acquired it was possible to walk for a mile along the parkland laced with paths and ponds while still being on the property.

The site, before becoming a college, had been owned by one of the richest women in Britain who had seventy people solely employed in tending and caring for the gardens and woodland.

Fortunately we had a horticultural genius on our staff in the person of Phil Hidderley who had tended our estates when we had been in Surrey and Cheshire. With just a team of four, though with mechanical equipment not at the disposal of the seventy gardeners of an earlier age, they do wonders.

When the various speakers had brought their presentations I opened the meeting for questions. Even though we suffered two short power failures during the meeting, we ensured all questions were answered and every possible fear allayed.

The meeting had gone well but even I was surprised by the final question which was, "Thank you for being so open and transparent about your intentions in the area. Could I ask that if you have any acts of worship on the site that we may possibly be allowed to attend?"

There are now two new Elim churches in the area – a small one that meets in West Malvern and an independent fellowship that asked to join Elim in Malvern itself.

When, many months later, the refurbishments were complete we invited all the local residents who wished to attend to join us for a buffet lunch and tour of the renovated complex and grounds. We wanted to express appreciation of the warm and generous way that they had 'invited us into their space'. We also asked, in order to mark this, if there was any way we could serve them as a community.

It was expressed that there was currently no facility in West Malvern to secure basic groceries or where people could meet their friends for coffee. We responded by converting part of our arts centre into a shop and coffee house. It is currently staffed partly by us and partly by local residents and has proved to be a helpful bridge with the community.

It is not widely known that Lord Baden-Powell made his decision to commence the Scouting movement while on what are now our grounds and there is an Edwardian orangery that marks the spot. He also laid the foundation stone for the primary building. The International Centre, college, conference and arts centre have proven to be a pivotal investment.

****

From time to time there were themes that I would teach across our network of churches and this was especially true of leadership days around the country. One of these was based upon the growth principles outlined in the parable of the fig tree in Luke 13.

It centred around the story of a tree that had been unproductive and the suggestion was that a process that included three specific stages be put into operation.

The first was that it be externally examined over time. The second was that digging be implemented to see if, below the surface, there were hidden reasons for lack of productivity such as the presence of rocks or stones.

If fruit still did not materialise the next stage was put in motion. The first stage had removed hindrances but stage two involved fertilisation. Stage one was about the removal of what should not be there and this stage was concerned with what was missing. If at this point growth had materialised then success had clearly been achieved.

If fruit did not occur then the next option took place – the removal of the tree from the ground so that what was non-productive did not take up space that could be better utilised by other things.

Though a church may have several areas in which it is fruit-bearing and productive there are often situations that are not. These then take up space in diaries, budgets and consume the limited resources of the personnel needed to keep them in place.

To 'remove obstacles in such situations' can be a matter of relocating individuals who, by their lack of ability or disposition, can be hindrances to productivity.

Fertilising, or adding nutrients, might parallel with financial investment or involve the relocating of the best people for the job into positions where they are most suited.

If a programme, department, ministry or institution fails to respond to any of these inputs it cannot make any sense, irrespective of how long it has been in place, to continue to let it take up space and resources any further.

Some people engage in attending expensive and time-consuming church growth seminars when sometimes what is really needed is the willingness to ask the hard questions and the courage to address unpalatable truths.

Another theme, closely allied to this that I asked our Movement to address – especially at local church level – had to do with 'gathering and scattering' factors.

In its simplest form gathering factors were the reason why people attended the church and why first-time visitors decided to stay.

Scattering factors, conversely, were the reasons why visitors chose not to make that congregation their spiritual home.

It's hardly rocket science to realise that if a church has more gathering factors than scattering it grows, and if it has more scattering factors it is going to decline.

When I first shared this some years ago at a meeting of *The Bridge*, the group that consisted of senior leaders who had congregations in excess of four hundred, one leader took the theme very much to heart.

He already had around a thousand people in his congregation and was about to take his own leadership away on a residential retreat. He later told me that he dispensed with most of the programme that had been previously planned in order to discuss what he now considered to be a greater priority.

After a period of time there were few leaders in Elim who were unaware of what came to be known as the 'Dig, Dung, Dismantle' concept.

Four Pivotal Events

It then occurred to me that if it was right to apply these principles to local church, did I have the courage to also apply the same criteria to everything we did at the highest levels of our Network.

Were we willing to ask ourselves the hard questions and, more importantly, having done so, implement them? What if we brought someone from outside our Movement to conduct the evaluation and allowed no ministry, budgetary consideration, or personnel to opt out of the analysis? Would we really take this parable that Jesus told as seriously as that?

I took this to my colleagues on the NLT and after much discussion we decided that this was the right course to set.

We approached someone who had been a top business analyst in the City. He was a committed Christian but by not being part of Elim had, we felt, the ideal impartial objectivity that was necessary.

To say that he was thorough was an understatement. He relocated from London during the week and spent five months scrutinising everything that we do, conducting countless hours of interviews and asking all the hard questions.

The good is often the enemy of the best. That we believed Elim was growing in size and depth did not mean that we should be reticent to look at ways in which we could grow further and faster.

There are always those who consider such exercises as unspiritual. Jesus was not one of them.

In the story of 'the feeding of the five thousand' the fact that there was a need and he had the answer were not considered by Jesus to be the only variables in the equation. He did not simply supply food indiscriminately. He managed the miracle by organising everyone into groups of fifties so that the supernatural would have clear and logical avenues of supply.

Henry Ford, the inventor of the mass produced motor car, said that he took the survival of the church in the world as proof of God's existence as no other enterprise run so badly could ever stay in business.

The Best is Yet to Come

It was Jesus who said that the *"Children of this world are wiser in their dealings with their own than are the children of light."*

The verbal report alone that Geoff Risdale brought to the NLT lasted for an uninterrupted one hour and fifty minutes apart from the auxiliary analysis that was printed for posterity.

This is not the place to outline the many facets of the report and the changes that were implemented. Mention should, however, be made of the fact that a highly qualified senior member of staff later joined us in the role as Executive Director of our operations based in Malvern. Alun Mathias has proved to be a valuable asset to our staff as has Sarah Bale who became our Administrator.

In 2012 we realised that Elim's centenary was just three years hence and so began to look at ways in which it might be celebrated. Chris Cartwright, at that time NLT member and Regional Leader for Wales and the South West, was asked to oversee the celebrations and did an exceptional job.

We had decided that celebrations would take place in several iconic venues around the UK and Northern Ireland. The NLT asked that I speak at all of these and I did so with the exception of Northern Ireland. I had been booked to speak at the Elim Conference in New Zealand on the date the Irish churches had selected. The speaker there was Malcolm Duncan and those who attended said that it, like all the other celebrations, was an excellent event. Around ten thousand Elim people attended one of the venues during the centenary year.

Other avenues of celebration were the production of a commemorative coffee-table book called *Defining Moments*. I well remember the day that Chris came to my home to show me the final draft and how it exceeded all my expectations. A thirty minute TV documentary was made that later became available on DVD and *Elim Sound* produced an excellent music album.

Three years earlier I was in no doubt whatever what it was that I wanted to 'bring to the party'. I referred to it as *'The Big Centenary Ask'* (TBCA).

Four Pivotal Events

I asked all of the churches in Elim to place 'church planting' on their agenda and consider committing to one of three things.

The first option was to plant a daughter church that would eventually become a church in its own right. The second option was to consider planting a multi-campus church. This would be a second congregation in the town or city that would remain under the direct covering of the central church. The third option was to consider planting a fresh expression of church.

There were many creative responses to this including Christian communities setting up with a coffee shop as its base and the planting of a church for surfers in France by Richard and Regi Ellerington.

Almost as soon as TBCA was launched a hundred and twenty churches opted for one of the three options and by our centenary year fifty-five brand new church plants were in the process of being pioneered.

Gary Gibbs leads REACH, our Evangelistic Department. I cannot commend him too highly for the time and energy he put into not just TBCA but also the pastoral care of church planters and the supplying of outreach resources. The more I got to know Gary and his wife, Sally, I found them to be of exceptional integrity and godliness.

By 2014 I was aware that I was in sight of end of my fourth term of office which would occur at our Conference in 2016.

Up to this point the procedure of selecting a successor was that, following the Conference at which the General Superintendent retired, the process to find a successor would be implemented. My predecessor for example stayed in office nine months after his term had ended to facilitate this.

I felt that I wanted things to proceed differently and so requested Conference two years earlier to change the procedure so that the selection of my successor could take place while I was still in office so that the passing of the baton could take place seamlessly at the Conference in which my tenure concluded. Conference agreed to this.

The Best is Yet to Come

I referred earlier in this book to what I called an 'embarrassment of riches' when it came to leadership calibre in the Elim Movement. This was also true at the level that was now under consideration.

The person eventually chosen was Chris Cartwright who received a strong mandate when the conference voted. The transition took place at the Harrogate International Conference Centre with over a thousand of our leaders present. Marilyn and I were greatly moved by the level of appreciation and affirmation we received as our role came to an end.

One of the greatest honours it has been my privilege to receive during my ministry came in 2016 when Marilyn and I were invited to Lambeth Palace to receive from the Archbishop of Canterbury the Lambeth Cross, the highest award that can be given to a non-Anglican. The citation that accompanied it said that it had been given for services to ecumenism in the United Kingdom.

Denominations are good but they are not for everybody. These days, as well as links with Elim, I work closely with newer Networks such as the Destiny Churches led by Andrew Owen, OneChurch Network led by Simon Jarvis and All Nations Network led by Steve Uppal.

This has been my story but your story is what really matters now. God has only got good plans for you and so for you, in the words of the *Elim Sound* anthem, *"The Best Is Yet To Come"*.

JohnGlass.co.uk

Appendix

Kilsyth – Heartland of Revival

There must be very few places on earth that have experienced as many significant moves of God as have occurred in Kilsyth, Scotland. In the past two hundred and fifty years this small town, with a population of under ten thousand, has experienced no less than three major revivals.

The Revival of 1742

The first revival occurred in 1742, a period in Scottish history that most would associate with Bonnie Prince Charlie. Just prior to the outbreak in Kilsyth, George Whitfield, writing in a letter dated July 19 records:

> *At mid-day I came to Cambuslang, and preached at 2pm to a vast body of people; again at 6 pm and again at nine at night. Such commotions surely were never heard of especially at eleven o'clock at night. For an hour and a half there was much weeping and so many falling into such deep distress, expressed in various ways as cannot be described. The people seemed to be slain in scores. Their agonies and cries were exceedingly affecting. Mr McCulloch preached, after I had done, till 1am in the morning; and they could not persuade the people to depart. In the fields all night might be heard the voices of prayer and praise.*

He refers to the scene in his writing as likened to a battlefield in which the wounded were supported by their friends as they were unable to stand unaided.

This revival was shortly to impact Kilsyth but, for the moment, we must step back ten years to encounter James Robe, the Kilsyth

Parish minister, a man who had preached to his congregation for over thirty years without any apparent success. During these years of apathy and lethargy Robe prayed earnestly for a descent of the Holy Spirit and had set up a seven year concert of prayer for revival.

In 1732 Kilsyth was stricken with a pleuritic fever which claimed sixty lives in just six weeks. A few months later devastating flooding swept away houses, drowned livestock and destroyed most of the cornfields. Eyewitnesses testify to hailstones falling which were three inches in circumference. Added to this, James Robe encountered opposition within his church and a number of people left. When famine ravaged the town and left people on the brink of starvation, it seemed that revival could not have been further away.

Robe, however, was tenacious and held on to God. His prayers were answered. Revival fires descended on the town. The impact of revival on society as a whole was soon felt. Because, however, there were many outward manifestations, strong wailing and falling down being two examples, Robe was charged with 'emotionalism'. Despite the fact that hundreds were saved, the religious establishment, as so often is the case, was unmoved by the power of God and spoke of the revival as a 'delusion and work of the Grand Deceiver'.

Robe answered his critics by pointing out that Satan's works never yet produced reformation of life and manners and the embracing of the righteousness of God.

The Revival of 1839

In the first quarter of the nineteenth century Kilsyth had hardened to the gospel to the point it was said that, "The Apostle Paul would not be able to get the people of Kilsyth out to a full meeting on three Sabbaths running."

However, this was to change. William Chalmers Burns, a young man twenty-four years of age, was led to preach on the subject of revival. He read from Acts 2 and then preached from Psalm 110:3,

'Thy people shall be willing in the day of Thy power'. As he ministered, people broke forth in uncontrollable wailing and tears and groans intermingled with shouts of joy and praise. Some screamed and others fell to the ground as if dead. The meeting eventually concluded at 3am having lasted five hours.

The revival had begun and, when he preached a few days later, he found himself preaching to a thousand people on a Saturday afternoon. The next day he preached for two hours to a crowd of ten thousand people. Another large service was planned that evening and yet another at 10pm. This meeting lasted till 3am. Some who had been counselled did not leave until 6am.

One man commenting on the impact of this move of God recorded, "The web became nothing to the weaver, nor the forge to the blacksmith, nor his bench to the carpenter, nor his furrow to the ploughman. They forsook all to crowd the churches and the prayer meetings." It was commonplace for hundreds to meet for early morning prayer in the market square before going to work.

Once again religious people opposed the move of God and, once again, the fruits bore eloquent and indisputable testimony to its genuineness.

Burns went as a missionary to China in 1846 and laboured there for over twenty years. He was a source of encouragement to the young Hudson Taylor who later founded the China Inland Mission. A missionary on furlough was asked if he had ever known William Burns, "Know him, sir?" he replied, "Every man in China knows him! He is the holiest man alive!"

Once again God had chosen to pour out His Spirit on the small town of Kilsyth but there were still more remarkable visitations yet to come.

The Revival of 1908

The *Kilsyth Chronicle* of June 12, 1897 announced meetings that would be taking place in the Westport Hall which were specifically intended 'to meet the wants of the non-church goer'.

At the turn of the century, poverty was rife in the town and Kilsyth had some of the worst housing stock in Britain during that period. Established churches in the town were having great difficulty integrating the largely mining community into church life. To their credit, local ministers supported the formation of a new fellowship and in 1902 a committee of four elders and four deacons was appointed. The designated name of the church was 'Church of God, Kilsyth'.

When revival fell in A.A. Boddy's church in Sunderland in 1908 one of the people who flocked to witness the Pentecostal outpouring was Bill Hutchison, an elder of the Kilsyth Church. This visit, together with the fact that A.A. Boddy made a timely visit to Scotland, generated a hunger in the hearts of a number of the Church of God leaders for an outpouring of God's Spirit. On 1 February 1908, the fire fell.

Between thirty and forty people were prostrated on the floor under the power of the Holy Spirit. Crowds flocked to the hall to see what was happening and those who could not get inside climbed up to the windows. In the weeks that followed two hundred people were baptised in the Spirit. Meetings were conducted every night of the week for four months. On a Sunday on which Cecil Polhill, one of the 'Cambridge Seven' who served with Hudson Taylor as part of the China Inland Mission, preached twenty-eight young people offered themselves for missionary service. The Church of God, Kilsyth became Scotland's first Pentecostal congregation.

* I am indebted to James Hutchison, author of the definitive work on the history of Kilsyth, *Weavers, Miners and the Open Book. A History of Kilsyth* for much of the historical detail mentioned in this article.

Other titles by John Glass

Building Bigger People

Open Heart, Open Hands

Saying No, Saying Yes

Released From the Snare

Amrach and the Paraclete

All available on Kindle at approximately £2.60 per title.